Be a Leader of Significance

BE
A LEADER
OF
Significance

Build Your Legacy,
Leave an Impact

Mosongo Moukwa

LIONCREST
PUBLISHING

BE A LEADER OF SIGNIFICANCE
Build Your Legacy, Leave an Impact

FIRST EDITION

ISBN   978-1-5445-4216-4 *Hardcover*
       978-1-5445-4215-7 *Paperback*
       978-1-5445-4217-1 *Ebook*
       978-1-5445-4218-8 *Audiobook*

To leaders who awaken the potential in others by shining their bright light.

CONTENTS

INTRODUCTION

In the early 2000s, Korn Ferry recruited me for a senior executive position at a paints and coatings firm based in India. When I interviewed for the position, they did not ask me to be a transformational leader. They wanted me to apply best practices to help establish their company as being an innovative organization. They were already a large player in Asia's vast paints and coatings market, and senior leaders saw no reason to pivot.

Once I began, I saw something different. The company was so entrenched in its status quo that it was missing out on the creativity that mid-tier employees wanted to bring to the table. How could innovation thrive in an environment where people did not have the tools or support they needed to explore creative opportunities?

At the same time, changes were brewing across the ocean. Organizations and governments were putting more emphasis on green, environmentally friendly alternatives to product portfolios. I knew these changes would soon impact the global paints and coatings industry and could sense an opportunity to build a strong, innovative organization—and leave a legacy in the process.

Over the next few years, the company went through a sizable transformation, none of which was in the works when I arrived. We came to own more than seventy new patents, and new products contributed roughly 10 percent to total sales. Productivity increased by 22 percent, and revenues more than doubled. We became the first India-based company to have a green portfolio of paints and the first to win one of the most prestigious awards in coatings technology for original scientific and innovative research.

The company's customers, suppliers, and competition actually began to recognize us for our innovation. This was notable since, a few years earlier, people had rarely thought of us as being innovative. We had successfully moved ahead of shifting dynamics and positioned ourselves as a regional and international market leader. Our people now sat on national boards and committees, and business magazines quoted them at length. Even years later, many of my former managers and employees continue to replicate this company's programs whenever they take leadership positions elsewhere.

These extraordinary results did not happen overnight or by accident. What made this possible? How could an organization with so many disengaged employees, most of whom were reluctant to ever go beyond their core tasks, become an engine for creativity? The path toward building this high-performing brand began by bringing the collective excitement and enthusiasm of team members from across the company's ecosystem into the fold of their larger mission and purpose. The end result was a complete organizational transformation—moving away from stagnation and toward becoming a creative center of experimentation that fueled sustainable revenues and growth that went beyond expectations. Among the key drivers involved is a different type of leadership.

Throughout my career, I have had the privilege to work at some of the world's top companies, helping them solve important innovation challenges. With this book you are reading, I look forward to sharing many lessons and successful practices to support you as you consider your own legacy and journey toward becoming a leader of significance.

WHAT IT TAKES TO BE A LEADER OF SIGNIFICANCE

Do you wish to unleash the creativity and energy of an organization? Do you want to help others achieve collective goals while giving people new ways to get energized? Are you prepared to make others a part of how you lead? Do you wonder how you can impact people in such a way that they remember these moments long after you have moved on? If so, then this is the work of a leader of significance.

A leader of significance makes a lasting difference and opens doors that lead to amazing results. My own journey in this direction started the moment I recognized that possibilities and opportunities exist in every interaction and conversation, regardless of job titles or positions.

Human connections and the quality of relationships you build determine how significant your leadership is. I have learned that in order to make extraordinary things happen, we must connect and associate leadership with the types of behaviors and actions that others see and recognize as possessing significance, purpose, and meaning.

To be a leader of significance requires you to have the courage to take your own path through this journey. To arrive at this type of leadership, you must dive deep into your own essence and discover new things about yourself. You will ask questions about your purpose, explore personal motivations, and define what legacy means to you. To truly rally people and inspire action, you must commit to your purpose, remain confident in your ability to achieve it, and inspire others to tap into their own confidence. This internal fulfillment will fuel your desire and ability to achieve even more.

As you go forward, you must willingly apply a sense of mission that lifts others and makes it easy and exciting for them to bring their best to your organization. You must commit to something bigger than yourself. That way, your goals will excite and inspire people around you. They will see them as being qualitative, tangible, and meaningful to the greater whole.

When you communicate with passion, others will want to join your efforts. When they see that your passion connects to your calling, they will make similar connections to their own and focus on things that matter. Your behavior and actions will show them that you care about them and that they are capable of achieving beyond their own expectations.

WHY BECOME A LEADER OF SIGNIFICANCE?

You may be thinking that this is all well and good, but why make the transition from being an effective leader to becoming a leader of significance? As a leader in today's world, you will not excite others just by promising them more money or by trying to encourage them to work harder to raise the company's share price. However, you will excite them when you encourage them to take aim at big goals—to innovate or create products that transform lives or to solve strategic challenges that others have failed to complete.

As a leader of significance, people will recognize your capacity to make a difference. They will follow you when they see that your dedication to a mission helps others find meaning and purpose in their work. When you tap into the hearts and minds of others with your words and actions, you will encourage them to reach higher and carry on when times are difficult. Through engagement and genuine acts of caring, you will reach many people in new ways.

Being a leader of significance will help you further your strategic standing in any company and exceed your financial performance. You will be able to move things around inside of your organization, experiment with new ideas, and disrupt processes in positive ways. It will help you attract new talents, customers, and partners and provide you with greater exposure for your ideas within and beyond the company. Soon you will likely find yourself a part of new forums that seek your contribution.

Your standing as a leader of significance will also encourage others to support your initiatives and help you make things happen. They will recognize you for your trustworthiness and the impact you have on people and teams. At the same time, the credibility of your team members will rise within your company as they continue to expand their confidence and skills.

The journey to becoming a leader of significance is not an easy one, and the lure of sticking with the status quo can be strong. Indeed, to become a leader of significance takes energy and risks, and the spotlight will be on you. Some people in your organization may even feel threatened by it. Why rock the boat? Why be bold when being good is often good enough? These types of questions come up for every leader. Sometimes they whisper in the backs of our minds. Other times, they keep leaders awake at night.

The fact is it takes courage to become a leader of significance—to move beyond the ordinary toward the extraordinary, revolutionary, and transformative. In the end, this work will most likely translate into greater recognition as you deliver on results, create positive impacts, and put a lasting, enduring culture into place.

Are you ready? I believe that the act of having read these first few pages is evidence that you are. So let me ask a few more important questions that this type of leadership brings to mind: Why are any of us here? What are we hoping to accomplish? What legacy do we want to leave behind?

While exercising this type of leadership, you will be driven by a sense of purpose—something that transcends the here and now, greater than anything anyone has achieved. This drive will come from within.

The more urgent truth is that today, executives need a different kind of leadership. Much has changed since I began my leadership journey in the early 1990s. Companies can no longer assume that leaders with traditional managerial skills will be successful in the C-suite. They need senior executives to motivate a diverse, technically competent workforce. In this dynamic, social and relationship skills are must-haves, as is the ability to rally and energize employees across the board.

THIS BOOK INCLUDES PRACTICES TO ASSIST YOUR JOURNEY

It's one thing to say, "Go unleash collective creativity." But how? And will doing so actually create tangible, measurable results your organization wants to see? The truth of my own career is that I did not envision becoming a leader but found myself in a leadership position in my earliest professional days.

Right away I faced a choice—to do what other leaders around me were doing or what I felt was best for the people I was leading and for the organization as a whole. I chose the latter and have never looked back. Along the way, I discovered a number of behaviors and actions a leader must take to operate at a personal best. I have included many of these throughout this book, grouped together into practices that start at the end of Chapter 2. Taken together, they represent an operating system for being a leader of significance.

Now in my fourth decade of leadership, I continue to seek ways to refine and implement new ideas that motivate people. I always come back to a foundational question: What topics, issues, or concerns naturally motivate people around me? Working from the energy of connection and understanding, I have found many paths toward leading larger organizational change. Over the years, I have developed principles and ideas to help executives successfully sharpen their leadership capabilities, all of which I look forward to sharing with you.

Throughout these pages, you will also find stories from my leadership journey across continents and organizational settings. If you follow them from chapter to chapter, they may inspire you to bring your own ideas to an organization, make an impact, and leave a meaningful legacy you are proud of. Through these stories, you will meet amazing people who have blossomed under this type of leadership, gain insights, and develop your own ideas about what it means to leave a lasting positive impact.

You will also discover that one of the best things to do as a leader is to find ways to listen and connect with people at all levels of an organization. Sometimes it's as easy as keeping your office door open, or making sure to stop in the break room at different times, or spending an extra five minutes talking over a cup of coffee.

The stories I will share do not exist in silos, nor are the themes related to doing things just to be different or fighting simply for the sake of the fight. In my own journey, reflecting on the story with which I started this book, the work was never just about creating new patents or commercializing innovative products. Instead, these outcomes were results of transformational change that started from the ground up.

As you'll find, these stories discuss aspects of developing teams, building upon disruption, tapping into innovative collective creativity, and harnessing potential to create lasting change.

They coalesce in a way to help you consider the following for your own leadership journey:

- Being on a mission
- Embracing experience and agility
- Seeking positive disruption
- Inspiring a shared vision
- Engaging with your teams
- Energizing the organization
- Creating opportunities for others
- Completing bold, innovative initiatives
- Enabling others to lead
- Unleashing organizational energy

I am sharing these stories and ensuing reflections in order to help you track your own as you think about your legacy and the impact you wish to leave behind.

HOW TO USE THIS BOOK

Please note that this is not a cookbook. You will not find recipes for instant success. Instead, you will discover practical insights that can help you guide and inspire, reflect and adapt, and ultimately unleash the potential of others—and of your organization—on account of your visionary leadership.

More than anything, this book is meant to be a guide you can read and return to throughout your journey. My intent is to explain what leadership of significance is and to share practices and examples that help you understand this type of leadership at a deeper, more meaningful level. The stories come from actual situations from my own leadership journey. As you read them, perhaps they will spur your own ideas. With that in mind, I encourage you to keep a pen and notepad, or a handheld recorder, handy to capture your own stories and memories.

Chapter 1 introduces you to the larger idea of leadership and contrasts being a leader of significance with a more traditional, transactional type of leadership. It serves to remind you that leadership is about relationships. Starting in Chapter 2, the book begins to explore the leadership practices I am advocating and shares stories associated with each. At the end of each chapter, I have included a series of action steps you can take today to steady your journey toward becoming a leader of significance. Finally, the book's conclusion offers a summary of thoughts to help you get started in a meaningful way.

THE WORLD NEEDS MORE LEADERS OF SIGNIFICANCE

Considering the current volatile and complex environment, where engagement is low and innovation is in high demand, a new type of leadership matters more than ever. My hope is that the work you do toward becoming a leader of significance helps to revitalize your workplace and enrich the lives of those you lead—and your life as well.

If you picked up this book because you want to amplify the impact of your leadership and make a difference in your organization, you will find that many of the practices will help you in your quest. If you think that pursuing leadership of significance can support you in your career, establish your credibility, and help build an organization that delivers beyond expectations, you will find many ideas to help you accomplish these goals. If you are a coach or a mentor, you will find ideas that can inspire those who seek your support. Finally, if you are already on your journey of being a leader of significance, this book will help you reflect on where you've been and where you're going next.

Ask yourself: What is at the heart of your motivation today? What energy exists behind your drive as a leader? If you could unleash the collective creativity of the people within your business, or even your department, how would their energy impact the present and future course of your organization?

YOUR LEADERSHIP LEGACY AWAITS

The world is filled with people who prefer to keep their heads down and avoid taking on anything too big, or bold, or risky. Luckily, it is also filled with those who follow the opposite track—who feel the friction in various circumstances and see opportunities waiting like light switches on the nearest wall of every dark room. If you are reading this book, I believe that you are from the latter camp—you actively think about change and are ready to take opportunities to create it.

Leaders of significance don't always start with a clear plan. We may stumble around sometimes or even lose our way. I know I have. So will you. Somehow, we find it again. Hopefully, the idea of leadership of significance energizes you. The key begins when you shift your mindset and break out of your traditional role in order to transform yourself into a fierce and earnest listener. When you do, what you will begin to hear may surprise you—employees at all levels of your organization are hungry for something more. Perhaps you are the person to guide them to it.

If you are willing to act boldly and put yourself in the center of your team—to be the ears they need and the guide they will follow—you will create the space for your organization to unleash its true potential. Doing so frees people from things that hold them back. When you unleash their confidence and creativity, you give them new eyes with which to approach opportunities with curiosity and to transform their own questions into tangible insights. What's more, you breathe fire into their ability to lead others along the way. As the energy perpetuates, one room's glow lights up another, then another, then another.

The idea of transformational change can be intimidating, but the reality of any change, no matter how small, is exhilarating. It becomes its own energy force, a light that flips on in the darkness, then breeds new light in its wake. Soon this light builds with a creative force that drives changes forward, shaking the status quo awake and completing actions that others may not have thought were possible.

Legacy is a tricky thing, and the nature of significant leadership rarely reveals itself as it happens. It tends to be something a person arrives at and recognizes over time. In many ways, your legacy is not about the results you achieve but the path you follow in achieving them. Certainly, your legacy will always involve your achievements. However, a more significant part of your legacy shows in the success and growth of the people you help, long after you move on.

If you achieve great results, but then things fall apart when you move on, then it is fair to say that you did not create enduring positive change. If you leave a company or enterprise and no one remembers you, then you have not touched the hearts and minds of employees, managers, and leadership peers. Like smoke, everything will have vanished into thin air.

Leadership of significance magnifies your influence. And, with that in mind, the first steps toward creating a lasting legacy include creating relationships of trust with those who look to you for guidance and support.

Perhaps you are at the start of your leadership journey, and you want to leave something better behind. Maybe you are a mid-career professional and are ready to embrace something bigger. Or perhaps you are reaching the end of your journey and find yourself reflecting on your own stories.

Do you wish to achieve something that no one has yet achieved? Do you want to develop new skills and leave an indelible mark on your organization? Most importantly, do you seek to leave a legacy that endures in the hearts and minds of other people? If you answered yes to these questions, then *Be a Leader of Significance* is for you.

Now is the time to continue your journey toward becoming a leader of significance. Let's begin!

Chapter 1

BEING A LEADER OF SIGNIFICANCE

How does one communicate their thoughts on what true leadership looks like? What makes leaders effective is building relationships through human connection. It is about creating an environment where people feel confident enough to bring their authentic, energized selves to work every day and to ask politely for what they want. Unless employees feel relatively safe, they will not risk speaking up. This is called psychological safety—a characteristic you find in many thriving workplaces. As a leader, you must create an environment where there is mutual trust. This is where I would like to begin Chapter 1.

DEVELOPING PEOPLE

One of the very first senior executives I worked with said to me, "Mosongo, we are not here to manage projects. The projects will get done. The most important thing we can do is to develop people."

When leaders focus on developing other people, they help them unleash their skills and creativity, and also strengthen the company in the process. This is a reminder that being a leader of significance is about more than developing people; it also involves moving the organization toward a common goal while making the experience meaningful for employees at personal and professional levels.

Leaders of significance take inspiration from various characteristics of servant and transformational leadership. While servant leadership focuses on the development of individuals within an organization, transformational leadership focuses on inspiring employees to move toward a common goal. This is the start to leaving a legacy and becoming a leader of significance.

MORE THAN TRANSACTIONAL LEADERSHIP

When leaders focus exclusively on managing projects, fulfilling responsibilities, and hitting numbers that others set for them, they are not stepping into the role of being a leader of significance. Instead, they are following a traditional leadership model. This may be safe and comfortable, but is it really what's best for the people they lead? Is it best for the company?

Most transactional leaders focus on maintaining the status quo and delivering results that will satisfy people up the chain. I have encountered many such leaders throughout my career. This is not a knock against them, as many traditional leaders are very good at their jobs—and also very good people. This transactional leadership calls for you to complete your role in exchange for a reward. In fact, most of us have some aspects of this as part of our leadership style because in a hierarchical organization, all of us have to perform.

Transactional leadership is a traditional mindset that leaves little room for creativity, inhibits growth, and dampens excitement among employees. It can actually create the wrong type of legacy, especially if lower-level employees are just trying to emulate what they see at the top.[1] If these employees don't see opportunities for creativity or innovation coming their way, why should they push for change or challenge themselves to develop new skills? Maybe if they stay in their boxes and continue to focus on the numbers, they too will earn a promotion, and maybe an office one day.

This reminds me of a story about an employee named Jim Lozinski, whom I had the pleasure to manage during the earliest stages of my career. I had just finished my PhD and taken a job with a specialty chemicals firm in Ohio. I was excited to be part of their research and development division and looked forward to settling into a career as a research scientist.

Not long after I started, the vice president of R & D called me in for a one-on-one meeting. After a few pleasantries, he sat forward in his chair. "Well, Mosongo," he said, "I see something more for you than hiding out in R & D. We're going to make you a manager."

I'd never managed people before and was caught off guard by this sudden announcement. "I'm not sure I'm ready to do this," I replied. "I have never managed any people." The VP was unbothered by my admission. "You'll be fine," he said.

1   Hemant Kakkar and Niro Sivanathan, "The Impact of Leader Dominance on Employees' Zero-Sum Mindset and Helping Behavior," *Journal of Applied Psychology* 107, no. 10 (2022): 1706–1724, https://doi.org/10.1037/apl0000980.

Suddenly I was a brand-new manager with no management experience and would have to figure things out. When I completed my research work at Northwestern University, I expected to work in a laboratory, design new products, and develop a strong intellectual portfolio. This was in the early 1990s, and the company did not have a mentorship program or any type of executive coaching model like things you see today. A few people helped me fill in various gaps, but I was more or less on my own. Whenever I brought a challenge to the VP, he repeated his favorite phrase: "Don't worry; you'll be fine." One year led to two, then to three, and eventually a long and very interesting career. And throughout everything, I have never regretted being in a leadership role.

One of the most challenging aspects of this situation was that the VP was actually quite controlling. Even though I credit him with giving me my first real opportunity to manage, reporting to him as a manager was not always the easiest thing to do. He enjoyed a strong grip over most of what happened in our organization, including how and to whom other managers and I assigned projects.

As time went on, I began to get a handle on a number of interpersonal workings. I found that the key for me involved building personal connections—something I mentioned in the introduction and that I will come back to again and again throughout this book. In fact, after only a few months as a manager, our department's productivity doubled. Of course the VP liked this since the numbers were his chief concern. During a managers' meeting, he looked up from his notes and said to our group, "Well, I'm not exactly sure what Mosongo is doing down at that end of the hall, but whatever it is, he should keep it up. It seems to be working."

Still, even with his vote of confidence, he continued to maintain control over how we distributed projects and whom we selected to lead initiatives. He certainly had his favorites and didn't bother being subtle about it. If he wanted Frank, or Chuck, or Henry to lead a project, then he would simply anoint them to do so, regardless of whether a manager had someone else in mind. In fact, he would regularly override managers in front of our group. It was another way to keep us all in our boxes and maintain the type of order he wanted to see.

One name that the VP never mentioned was *Jim*. Among my R & D group, I recognized that Jim was a very hardworking and intelligent scientist, perhaps one of our group's brightest minds. Still, the VP thought very little of Jim and did not see him as someone who would grow as part of our organization. Whenever I mentioned Jim in a meeting, the VP would push the idea aside and call out a name of his liking.

Toward the end of my first year as a manager, our company launched an initiative to explore key new technologies. Eventually these technologies would cycle into our portfolio, and the work of selecting them would be highly detail oriented. The VP tasked me with building a team from the R & D group to lead this initiative, knowing full well that we would be incorporating these new technologies into our platform.

I sat in my office, wondering whom to give the project to, when I heard someone coming down the hallway. The footsteps slowed as they approached my door. It was Jim. He stood in the threshold for a moment, knocked on the opened door, and asked if he could come in. "Of course," I said. "What is on your mind?"

"Well," he said. "I've heard about this new project and wanted to know if you've chosen a lead yet."

"I'm still working on that," I said. "Do you have someone in mind?"

"Yes." He perked up. "I would like to lead this project. I looked at the requirements, and I know I can do it. I'd appreciate it if you consider me."

"Let me think about it," I agreed. After Jim left my office, I thought, "Yes, why not Jim? Of course I should give him this chance." After that, all I had to do was to figure out how to navigate the VP's reluctance. He would certainly have an issue.

A few days later, during our weekly managers' meeting, the VP asked if I had made my choice for the project lead. I could see he'd already written out a list of familiar names on his notepad.

"Yes," I said. "I've given it to Jim." The VP's face went red. "Jim?" he asked in disbelief.

I looked around the room. The other managers diverted their eyes toward the papers in front of them. They knew the VP had issues with Jim. They also knew, as did I, that he held grudges. Had I just signed my own pink slip?

The meeting went on as scheduled, and the VP said very little to me. Afterward, he pulled me aside. "I think you should reconsider this," he said. "I'd like Frank to lead this. Shall we go with Frank then?" It wasn't really a question so much as it was a life jacket. He was giving me one last chance not to drown and also reminding me that he was in charge.

"Frank is a great worker," I said, "but Jim is the right person to lead this project. We'll go with Jim."

"Suit yourself," he replied and briskly left the room.

MAKING AN EMOTIONAL CONNECTION

So much hinges on trust—building it, communicating it, and extending it over time. It's a fragile thing, and you certainly do not want employees, or other senior managers or leaders for that matter, to lose it once you've developed it.

It's also important to remember that a leader must possess trust in him or herself as well. Perhaps this seems obvious, but then again, maybe you have not thought about it in some time. If you have risen to a certain point of leadership in your career, then you have no doubt crossed many thresholds that led to trust. Maybe years ago, you rapped on someone else's door and asked for a chance. Or maybe it was you who said yes and then advocated for them.

Exhibiting trust is not about bragging or showing a false sense of elevated confidence, like throwing your weight around. In this story, I only knew what I knew: that Jim was eager and that the VP would dislike the decision. Jim came to me because he trusted me. I believed he was capable, but I knew he would need support.

What I am talking about here is a type of self-trust or self-confidence that actually shows up as humility in action. Carrying this type of quiet confidence can be key when you are trying to win someone over, get to know someone, or find ways to connect with people so you can help them gain their own levels of self-confidence. Leaders who evoke this type of quiet self-confidence are often seen as warm, interested, empathetic, and eager to learn more about the people around them. They are more interested in asking questions and listening than they are in talking about themselves or bragging about their accomplishments.

On the other side of this conversation is the type of leader who feels the need to lead with his or her accomplishments first. This leader is less interested in building connections and more focused on talking big. These leaders may show up as arrogant, but they actually possess low confidence, and they must constantly talk themselves up and remind you who is in charge.

Humility, trust, and quiet self-confidence cycle back to support you on your leadership journey. When you exhibit them, you help amplify similar values and traits in others. You let them know that they don't have to be the loudest person in the room in order to be seen and recognized for their accomplishments and energy.

GIVE OTHERS THE CHANCES THEY SEEK

One thing I have discovered during my career is how important it is to give other people chances, especially when they advocate for themselves. Jim understood the protocol of our company and was well aware of the fact that the VP did not see much in him. But he was confident in his abilities and trusted that I shared this confidence. Was I actually staking my career on Jim's success? At the end of the day, it's a moot question, because Jim was successful in this venture.

Hungry employees often rise to the occasion, especially when they voice their desire beforehand. But how will they discover their potential if they remain unseen? If they cannot discover and put their potential to use, the company will also miss out.

In this experience, I was able to give Jim the space and latitude he needed to grow into a new version of his professional self. No one knew what he was capable of until he had the opportunity to take something on that was a little bigger than what he was already doing. When Jim came to my office that day, he was reluctant to ask for what he wanted, uncomfortable shining the light on himself. He needed someone to switch the light on for him in order to breathe life into his aspirations. He was certainly qualified, but this was an opportunity for him to level set and then level up.

This experience wasn't just important for Jim, but also for me. It became a type of fuel for me that I relied on at different times in my career, especially in those moments when I recognized a similar yearning among employees who also wanted to prove themselves. I reflected on this experience in Ohio quite often, because it wasn't just about developing new talent. It was also about steering the company in exciting new directions.

REFLECTIONS

As a leader of significance, you create a foundation for confidence that leads to new and exciting things—for your people, your company, and yourself. You motivate people to achieve something that matters to them and to the company as a whole. To do so, you must be willing to create opportunities in which others can thrive, even if it means putting yourself out on a bit of a limb. Once out there, you must become a bridge that covers the gap between the opportunities they crave and the potential they wish to exhibit and achieve.

Many leaders of yesterday fell into the category of being a know-it-all or central go-to person—someone who needed to put their stamp on everything, much like the VP in this story. However, leaders who care about legacy are motivated to mobilize the intellectual and emotional capabilities of the organization. Doing so helps to achieve the company's goals while also helping individuals sharpen their capabilities so that they can make an impact. Meanwhile, such leaders do not need credit or recognition. They strive to help others find new ways to apply their talents in order to help the organization grow.

Leadership is not about the title you hold. It's about building relationships and expanding the quality of those relationships in the process. When you put emotional connection at your foundation, you begin to discover what people are capable of. It was easier for me to advocate for Jim because he and I had built a strong rapport during my first year as his manager. I saw beyond the projects and understood the person, including his needs and concerns. Nurturing this type of awareness and understanding is vital. Without the human connection, there isn't much else to lean into or build from. Once you develop such a connection, you can then move employees toward the common goals.

Being a leader of significance is also about helping people discover their potential, or even rediscover a potential they have forgotten. You must invest the time it requires to get to know your people and understand what they are capable of. Then you can put them in positions where they can prove themselves to others. In the process, you must also be there for guidance and support when they need it.

I worked closely with Jim as he led this major project. We built a strong roadmap, kept our eyes on the goal, and presented the type of hard data that the VP wanted to see. As the project went on, I slowly stepped away but continued to engage him. Jim maintained a fantastic grasp on what needed to happen at every phase.

The confidence I showed in Jim by investing time in his development increased his own confidence, made him feel more engaged in his work, and ultimately improved his performance. He turned out to be one of the most productive people in the organization, called upon to lead strategic key projects and contributing beyond his own expectations to the achievements of the organization.

As a leader of significance, you will be exerting a type of leadership known as "servant leadership," where leaders put themselves in the service of others, regardless of where people exist on the org chart. The main characteristics of servant leadership include "listening, empathy, healing, awareness, persuasion, conceptualization, foresight, stewardship, commitment to the growth of people and building community."[2]

---

2   Larry C. Spears, "Character and Servant Leadership: Ten Characteristics of
     Effective, Caring Leaders," *Journal of Virtues & Leadership* 1, no. 1 (2010):
     25–30, https://www.regent.edu/journal/journal-of-virtues-leadership/
     character-and-servant-leadership-ten-characteristics-of-effective-caring-leaders/.

Servant leadership implies that you are here to help other people strengthen their own capabilities so they apply their talents in ways that make an impact and help the organization grow. It creates an empowering experience for the followers and releases a lot of energy. In the words of Laozi, the Chinese philosopher, "A leader is best when people barely know he exists; when his work is done, his aim fulfilled, they will say: we did it ourselves."[3]

By employing this type of leadership while also pursuing the collective goals of the organization, you ensure that those you lead will remember more than just your financial achievements; they will also remember what you have achieved on their behalf and how you made them feel. They will remember the fire you lit in them.

At the end of the day, your leadership legacy is not about leaving something for people, but something in people. You want to do something of significance for the community, your organization, and your followers. This is because of the way you consistently behave, the confidence you exude, the character you display, and the compassion you show to others. In this type of leadership, the leader and the followers move each other to a higher level of motivation and energy.[4] That is why you must make each day count.

---

3   Michael Shinagle, "The Paradox of Leadership," Harvard Division of Continuing Education: Professional Development, July 3, 2013, https://professional.dce.harvard.edu/blog/the-paradox-of-leadership/.

4   George P. Allen et al., "The Role of Servant Leadership and Transformational Leadership in Academic Pharmacy," *American Journal of Pharmaceutical Education* 80, no. 7 (2016): 1–7, http://dx.doi.org/10.5688/ajpe807113.

LET US GET STARTED

There's a good chance that you are already leading in your current position. The exercises that follow will help you reignite your passion for a type of leadership that makes an impact and that others will remember for years to come. As you begin, I recommend that you reflect on the type of leader you would like to be and the type of leadership that you envision for yourself.

1. **Reflect on experiences that molded your leadership.** To succeed in leadership, the idea of caring for others must be in our hearts. Reflect on experiences (planned or unplanned) that have shaped you and revealed your distinctive abilities. What were they and what did you discover? List the times when you felt most fulfilled. This will help you rekindle your passion.

2. **Write your future self.** Envision the leader you know you could be. Envision that future. Think of all the ways you would like to be remembered. In that future, how many lives did you positively impact? What is the inner voice or impulse urging you to do at this point in your life's journey? What are you practicing every day to mentally progress toward the desired future?

Chapter 2

BE ON A MISSION

As a leader of significance, you must have the courage to follow journeys where they take you, especially when a mission lands in your lap. In fact, only when you step into your mission completely, with your full self, can you begin to inspire others to step up and help you achieve the same goals. You must be committed to something bigger than what's in front of you and to following through in order to excite and inspire. This is the energy with which I would like to start Chapter 2.

STARTING SOMETHING NEW

In 2002, I learned about a new VP position with a firm in North Carolina. They were in the US, a subsidiary of a larger Japanese firm. Their focus was the development of polymers used in high-end automotive coatings. After a few interviews, I felt a strong connection with their hiring team and was excited to sit down with the CEO near the end of the hiring phase. Over dinner, I asked him how he intended to judge whether or not I would be a successful hire.

"We have spent more than a decade trying to transfer a key technology from our parent company in Japan," he said. "We have failed every time, for reasons I won't bother to get into. Your top priority will be to bring this technology to our operations in the States. Do you think you can get it done?"

"I will certainly try," I said.

The CEO leaned forward across the table. "To be honest with you, Mosongo, in the eyes of our parent company, our division is bleeding money. This transfer is more than the key to our success. It's the bridge to our survival. And without it..."

"I think I understand now."

"You see, I've had others say they will try," the CEO went on. "I would like you to be the person who actually does make this happen. And that is how I will judge your success in this position. Now do you understand completely?"

"Yes," I nodded.

"For you to be successful, you will need to develop personal and professional relationships with the Japanese," he said. "Are you prepared to do that?"

"I am."

FROM GOAL TO MISSION

The technology transfer from Japan was much more than a passion project for the CEO. The stakes could not be higher.

As far as the Japanese parent company was concerned, our US operations were simply not profitable, at least not to the point where they needed us to be in order to stay on their books. However, if we could bring some of their technologies in-house, it would create a cascade effect and lead to net profits across many aspects of the company.

With the new technology in place, our firm could develop an entirely new portfolio among high-end automotives. This would open doors to manufacturing plants all throughout North America. The senior leaders in Durham knew that time was of the essence and that the parent company was prepared to begin cutting losses.

I was determined to change the spirit and approach that the organization had previously taken with respect to acquiring the technology from Japan. Right away, I met with my new team to get a sense of what we were capable of and where we would need support. I also wanted to talk with team members who had been involved in the previous attempts to bring this technology over from Japan. Most of what they shared seemed to put the emphasis on their Japanese counterparts.

"They're difficult to work with," one team member said. "They would give us part of what we needed, but not all of it, no matter how many times we asked. After a while, we stopped asking."

"What about the time before that?" I asked.

"It was the same thing," he said.

"And the time before that?" I countered.

"Also the same," he said.

The work we needed to do wasn't just about our capabilities. Yes, of course we had to be sure we possessed the right technical infrastructure. But more than anything, we needed to foster a stronger connection and better communication if we were going to make this work.

I continued to dig into the past. What else had or had not happened in those previous experiences? What stumbling blocks had occurred? What bridges simply did not extend far enough? I soon learned that previous senior leaders who had attempted this transfer had rarely traveled to Japan in order to meet the people on the other side. To me, that was a major gap. This was long before businesses could rely on video conferencing in order to make a face-to-face connection. Plenty of people were still communicating via fax as much as email, if you can believe that. Things had to change.

When I met with the CEO for an update, I shared this critical piece of information. "Well," he said, "it looks like you're going to Japan."

I began to develop a sense of mission, accomplishing something that has not been achieved yet. Having that sense of mission also helped me continue to learn when faced with challenges. Those who exercise leadership are propelled by a sense of mission.

BEING THE STRANGER

While transferring the technology, the goal was qualitative, tangible, important, and meaningful. Still, in the beginning, the people on the US side of the operation were not all that excited about it, especially those who had been down this path before. They saw the hurdles in front of them, and even when they could clear the hurdles, the past continued to haunt them. I had to find a way to drive forward with passion and conviction and to focus the collective energy toward achieving this mission.

I had never visited Japan before and did not know even the smallest bit of the language. My counterparts were extremely warm and inviting and went out of their way to help me acclimate and adjust to the new surroundings. They were well aware of how determined I was to make this technology transfer happen. Still, despite my determination and the fact that time was of the essence, I did not want to convey a sense of haste or to come across as abrupt. I was focused on building connections—getting to know them and giving them a chance to get to know me as well.

For the next few weeks, as we got to know one another, I also learned their perspective as to why the transfer had failed in the past. One of the main issues pointed back to the differences in regulations between the types of chemicals and processes the Japanese could use and how things translated in the US. There were a great number of variables to adjust to make things work in the States. As I unpacked these details, I again saw that a missing ingredient was connection and communication. People on both sides had gotten hyperfocused on the pieces of the project—the data and details—but had forgotten the essential human links. Shortly before I flew back to North Carolina, a Japanese colleague threw his hands up during a meeting.

"Your country put a man on the moon but cannot figure this transfer out," he said. "Why?'

RALLY OTHERS TO A BIGGER MISSION

A mission cannot just be about you. It must be about something bigger—the people, the company, and even the future. It's impossible to get people excited about a mission where the goal is just to "raise the share price." It must be big but also tangible, important, and meaningful. People must be able to see that what you do—and what they do—counts. In this situation, the mission, from a broad perspective, was to do something that no one had yet achieved within this company. I had a vivid understanding of the mission and stakes involved.

Narrowing it down, the mission was also critical to the survival of the firm itself, which meant that the livelihoods of hundreds of people were at stake. It was time to rally my people in a new way.

My mission had started with, "We're going to make this happen; it is good for us and the company." After weeks of investigation, I knew that I needed to amplify my energy to the point of becoming an evangelist to this cause. I wanted there to be no doubt exactly what the mission was and why it mattered—not just to me, but to them. Plus, I wanted everyone to know that it would indeed take dozens of people on two different continents who spoke different languages to make it work.

The message I began preaching was that we had an opportunity to really transform the organization by finally bringing this technology over from Japan. It was no longer about responding to the CEO's challenge, nor about the failed attempts of the past. It was now about the future state.

"The technology is over there," I said at a meeting, pointing east.

"The talent lives on both sides of the world. What we need now is to build a bridge. If we can build one together, we will reach the future as a team." I repeated this message over and over again. I talked individually to some, and to others in a group setting.

Naturally, there were challenges, as there will always be when trying to accomplish something that is truly transformative. Rallying people to the cause was only one part of the equation. On a day-to-day basis, the true test came in the work itself. No longer were people getting swept up by the details or focused only on plugging numbers. Instead, they needed to equate each of their small tasks to the much larger mission-driven meaning. It did not matter if there were regulatory hurdles, trials to test, or errors to correct. I challenged colleagues to set deadlines for small steps. They began to see the reasons behind every step, which continued to point to the bigger mission.

Within this mix, we found new ways to challenge ourselves. If a team member thought they could accomplish a certain step in five days, we would wonder aloud as a group, "Can it be done in three?" People were encouraged to push themselves—to prove that they were up for the challenge and had a stake in its outcome. More than anything, we wanted to show what we were capable of.

At the same time, we needed to pace ourselves, especially when we hit challenges and delays. Despite the ticking clock, things could only move so fast. Stalls occurred for any number of reasons, often related to compliance issues that were beyond our control. Sometimes we simply had to wait to hear back from a government agency. Then we would press on in our ongoing attempt to pair the Japanese formulations with US compliance regulations.

What became one of the most critical aspects of the project, especially in those moments when we hit a wall, was knowing that our Japanese counterparts were truly rooting for us to make this work. We had successfully built the connections that had been missing during previous attempts. One gentleman in particular, Mr. Takeo, who was nearing retirement, stepped in and made it his mission to help me accomplish mine. In my back-and-forth trips to Japan, he took me under his wing, made sure I was comfortable, and galvanized his people in much the same way as I was attempting to galvanize mine.

REFLECTIONS

When you are given or take on a strategic goal, you must come out very powerfully in a way that others will follow. As a leader of significance, you must be willing to seize your role with focus and encouragement. As you do, you model and create a space for creative collective intelligence. You not only share your ideas, but you welcome the ideas of others. Obviously, you must follow through effectively.

The technology transfer took more than eighteen months to complete. With each move forward, my team and I delivered key metrics related to our progress, actions, and activities. Our work helped the company introduce a series of new products for the industrial and automotive markets, and the CEO continued to applaud our efforts.

Being a person on a mission is not easy work. Keeping others engaged and excited is always a challenge. You must have courage to take this type of journey. For a leader of significance, in order to truly dedicate yourself to drive your initiatives, you must believe that you and your people can achieve them. No one will follow you if you don't believe it yourself. Looking back at my own journey, I believe that to rally others around a goal or a mission, you must show courage, passion, and commitment.

This step is rarely easy. People may not understand your crusade or what you're trying to achieve, especially at the beginning. Some may worry that you are too intense about it. Sometimes it takes time to find the right words to communicate what's happening and why it must happen. It can be uncomfortable, but if you are a leader of significance, then you know that the greater discomfort is continuing to do things the same way in which others have tried and failed. You have to step out and expose who you really are and what you believe in. To do so, you must engage deeply and honestly with your people. Perhaps you will have to step back and let others lead, or let them help, in order to achieve something that no one else has done. And you will have to trust that the team around you are the people who will finally do it.

Inspiring and motivating those who follow your lead while also modeling a positive attitude are essential ingredients of the leader's charisma. In the book *Leading with Emotional Courage*, the author talks about being fully immersed in your mission, being confident and courageous.[5] This will assure a powerful presence, especially when you act boldly and powerfully.

Your passion and commitment can inspire others to join your cause. This passion shows itself when you are connected to your calling and invites others to connect to theirs. With your passion as an ally, you can rally people and inspire action.

---

5   Peter Bregman, *Leading with Emotional Courage* (Hoboken: John Wiley & Sons, 2018).

Passion is contagious. If you want to inspire your team, it starts with passion—a requirement if you wish to turn your mission into a reality. To inspire and sustain passion among employees, you need to express genuine enthusiasm and keep them excited about what you are all trying to accomplish together. You may even need to be loud at times. Research shows[6] that we tend to follow people who are enthusiastic and radiate energy—people with positive attitudes.[7]

You must show perseverance, especially when you face challenges and obstacles. Perseverance is a key ingredient for reaching achievements that lie ahead. It relates to your ability to stick with goals and tasks. Leaders who want to move people demonstrate personal drive and are persistent as they pursue a mission. They not only want to move the needle, but they do the work involved.

Such drive comes from within, and this determination keeps people focused. Angela Duckworth, author of *Grit: The Power of Passion and Perseverance*, argues that perseverance, combined with passion, is known as grit. To develop grit, a leader must cultivate a growth mindset and encourage perseverance.[8]

To be on a mission, you must also possess a future mindset. This is the opposite of having a narrow, fixed mindset that stays stuck in the past or lets the hurdles in front of you get to be too big. You must see the opportunities that exist in the distance and galvanize support as you go toward them collectively.

6   Daniel Goleman, *Social Intelligence: The New Science of Human Relationships* (New York: Bantam, 2006).

7   Belle Linda Halpern and Kathy Lubar, *Leadership Presence: Dramatic Techniques to Reach Out, Motivate, and Inspire* (New York: Gotham Books, 2003).

8   Angela L. Duckworth, *Grit: The Power of Passion and Perseverance* (New York: Scribner, 2016).

This future mindset is extremely important in today's world, where things are more volatile than ever. The nature of work and communications is rapidly changing and will continue to do so. If your mindset becomes too fixed or narrow, you will not be able to respond with the type of agility and foresight that you need—that which will benefit your company and the people who look toward you for leadership.

When you're a leader on a mission that others believe in, the whole organization moves forward toward shared goals. This is a difficult step, but you are ready to take it. It is about the idea of making a positive impact on people's lives and having the passion to be significant.

LET US GET STARTED

A mission is not something that someone else assigns, but something that you assign to yourself.[9] When you are on a mission, you are fiercely determined in pursuit of a specific, important, and significant goal. By aligning time and energy around it, your passion becomes contagious.[10] As a result, you will have more impact and draw more people to your cause.[11] I recommend some actions to help you enhance your competence in the practice of being on a mission:

---

9   Alex Lickerman, *The Undefeated Mind: On the Science of Constructing an Indestructible Self* (New York: Simon and Schuster, 2012).

10   Sylvia Hubner, Matthias Baum, and Michael Frese, "Contagion of Entrepreneurial Passion: Effects on Employee Outcomes," *Entrepreneurship: Theory and Practice* 44, no. 1 (2019): 1–29, https://doi:10.1177/1042258719883995.

11   Ke Wang, Erica R. Bailey, and Jon M. Jachimowicz, "The Passionate Pygmalion Effect: Passionate Employees Attain Better Outcomes in Part Because of More Preferential Treatment by Others," *Journal of Experimental Social Psychology* 101, no. 1 (2022): 104345, https://doi.org/10.1016/j.jesp.2022.104345.

1. **Identify your mission.** Discovering a mission involves finding pursuits that are worthy to focus on and drive. Missions are about recognizing the intrinsic worth of tasks. Assess problems in your organization that are worthy of your energy, especially those that, if solved, will leave a lasting impact on the company and your customers. Transform your goal into a mission. With a mission in hand and with your skills, you are now determined to pursue it.

2. **Communicate constantly.** Communicate your mission expressively. Engage and enroll followers. A confident leader is remembered as one who made others feel empowered. Experiment with the potential mission. This gives a purpose and builds momentum. Start small and evolve into an evangelist.

Chapter 3

EMBRACE EXPERIENCE AND AGILITY

In Chapter 2, I discussed the need for a leader to show emotional courage in pursuit of goals. Here in Chapter 3, I'd like to explore another characteristic that a leader of significance must possess: learning agility. It is a combination of mental agility, people agility, change agility, results agility, and self-awareness. The story I will share below involves challenging context and exemplifies the importance of learning agility in one's leadership journey.

GETTING TO THE CORE OF LEARNING AGILITY

When you are in the midst of building an organization, following through on a mission, or just trying to keep your head above water in an unlucky scenario, you might also find yourself navigating a complex business world. In such situations, you must be adaptable, resilient, and open to new ways of thinking.[12] In your journey, it helps when you draw from past experiences and moments of learning agility.

Learning agility is about discovering what you have the potential to accomplish when you face challenges. No doubt you have acquired many skills over the years, along with capabilities from which you draw again and again. Possessing a mindset where learning agility matters makes it easier for you to draw upon them, especially when you face challenges. Learning agility is a set of attributes that allows you to stay flexible, grow, and rise to a range of challenges. It is one of the most important competencies for any leader to possess. Learning agility has helped me get through tricky situations.

MOVING FORWARD WITH THE HELP OF THE PAST

In the year 2000, I accepted a VP position with a Wisconsin firm that specialized in a number of consumer products. This wasn't my first move, but it was the first for my growing family, as my wife and I had children by then.

The prospect of starting a new chapter in my career was exciting, and the company represented an opportunity to be exposed to new technologies and develop skills within a new industry. During the interview, I made a strong connection with the CEO, a gentleman named Mike Hoefflin. He informed me that a gentleman named Olaf Schoen, who currently held my position, would be moving over to manufacturing, where the CEO

---

12   David F. Hoff and David E. Smith, "Leadership and Learning Agility: A Lifelong Journey for W. Warner Burke," *The Journal of Applied Behavioral Science* 56, no. 4 (2020): 492–502, https://doi:10.1177/0021886320954922.

thought he'd be better suited. The CEO hoped that I would be able to help invigorate the division's innovation activities, eventually making a push toward more innovation, which had stagnated. In his view, after experiencing annual growth of 10 percent for a number of years, things had stalled. He was worried and wanted new energy and insights to help turn things around.

With the new job ahead of me, I finished my career in Ohio on a positive note and dove into the tasks involved in moving. A few days before starting, I received a call from the recruiter who first opened the door to the Wisconsin opportunity.

"Mosongo, I take it you are excited about starting soon," he said.

"Very much so," I said. "Is everything okay?"

"Well, there's been a change," the recruiter said. "It seems that Mike, who hired you, is no longer CEO. There's been a shake-up. I thought you would like to know."

STARTING ON ROCKY GROUND

As I came to discover, the new CEO had been with the company for a long time but had been based in Europe. The rumors were that he pushed the previous CEO out. Still, I was determined to make the best of things. It was too late to turn back—I'd finished my work in Ohio, and our family was already halfway moved in. I started at my new position a few weeks before the new CEO arrived and quickly went to work getting to know my group and building connections in the way that had helped me help others in the past.

Even though I hadn't met the new CEO yet, I was already hearing whispers—people love to gossip, especially when there's been a mysterious power play in the works. "He's brutal," someone told me. "He's an outsider. He doesn't like what's going on here."

"It's going to be bad," someone else said. "When you have your first performance appraisal, he will absolutely cut you to pieces."

I let these rumors slide. It was better not to dwell on what I did not know. When we finally met after three weeks, I soon understood why people felt this way.

"Mosongo," he said, not looking up from his desk, but staring at a copy of my résumé in his hand. Then he set the résumé down, folded his hands, and cleared his throat. "I'll be very direct. My predecessor hired you. I did not. He's no longer here, and I'm in this chair. I have different goals than he did. He wanted to innovate. I want to reorganize your entire group and focus on new business development. That involves moving most of your people in the US away from technology development and into the new business development division. This is the metric on which I'll judge you. You will still have the groups in Europe and some here in the US. But, honestly, if I had been here two months ago, we would not have hired someone from outside the company. That is all."

The new CEO had effectively made a bet on this plan. He wanted to shift the focus of the company's US-based division over to new business development, in the hopes of reversing eroding profitability. My first thought after walking out of his office was, "How in the world will this work? It is going to be a challenge in this environment."

SWITCHING GEARS

In three weeks, my role had completely changed and appeared diminished from what I had come to do. The experience presented two distinct roads to follow. I could quit, or I could switch gears. Should I quit? Probably. Could I quit? No. My growth mindset would not allow it.

For the next three months, I buried myself in work but also kept my head up in an effort to build the types of human connections that I knew mattered more than anything else. Starting in a new industry is never easy. Operating in that particular environment made the entire experience feel like walking a minefield. I wondered whom to trust, where to find answers, or how to get the help I needed. Once someone sees you as being a poor fit for a team, it becomes that much harder to have your work recognized. I wanted to prove that I could be an outlier rather than succumb to the stress of the new leadership regime. To do so, I remained open and engaging.

An interesting light bulb clicked on for me. Perhaps innovation was the key to creating new business. I could effect change by doing what I'd been hired to do: drive innovation forward, even though the context had changed. I could pay attention to the new CEO's prescriptive guidance, adapt my workflow to meet his expectations in a highly visible way, and put my emphasis on meeting his priorities.

As far as my relationship with the CEO was concerned, I knew I could not bank on his support, at least not wholeheartedly. He would judge me exclusively on my performance, based on the lens he had decided to look through. Every move I made would fall under the specter of his second-guessing. Luckily, there were other managers and leaders who understood the political scenario that was taking place. Some lent me the support I needed. That included Olaf, who had moved into a new position when I came on board, as well as an HR manager who inducted me into the inner workings of the company.

One thing I knew about myself was that I was capable of learning and could lean on my years of research and development experience, along with my MBA in marketing and finance, as much as necessary. I didn't know a lot about their technology base at first, so I asked Olaf if he would be willing to help me get up to speed. He was more than happy to help. He and I spent extra hours hunkering down as I learned as much as I could in fairly short order. With his support, I also began learning more about their various consumer markets. I oversaw the processing and technology development groups in Europe and the company's extensive IP portfolio, which they were spending upward of $1 million to maintain.

In this stretch of difficulty, I discovered new ways to learn an entirely new set of capabilities. I also expanded my arsenal of knowledge related to the processing technology of special chemicals, mergers and acquisitions, technology licensing, and the mangagement of intellectual property. The company was extremely active in seeking to acquire materials and polymer technologies, which provided a fertile ground for learning. And I also continued to develop a strong connection with a handful of managers.

When I reflect back on this situation now, I understand that I moved into a growth mindset. At first, it was a mechanism that helped me cope; in hindsight, it also helped me learn new skills that I would use in the future.

In order to develop a growth mindset, leaders must embrace challenges, persist, and recognize that their efforts create a path toward mastery. When people face challenges, they can easily become insecure or fearful. There will always be discomfort when learning new things. Once I stepped out of the space of frustration, I was able to start learning. In the end, this provided me with a great deal of energy. None of the positives would have happened if I had given up. I would have lost much more than education—I would have missed out on the type of growth that comes from experiencing challenging situations.

This experience also helped discover the type of environment in which I can thrive. It helped me learn about myself and find out what it means to be authentic. Also, I had to unlearn various things in order to free myself from the trap of expectations and shift toward new competencies. The entire experience was an exercise in learning agility.

REFLECTIONS

I am certain that you have faced a wide range of challenges in your life. Hopefully, each challenging experience equipped you with new skills, abilities, knowledge, and insights you can integrate as you pull from lessons you have learned that apply to a current situation. From these experiences, you can select information or tools and make a relevant comparison to other situations as they are happening. Doing so may present you with the exact information you need, thereby increasing your capacity for effective leadership.

However, merely having an experience is not enough. Also important are the lessons you extract from the experience and how you apply them to future situations.[13] First, to uncover these lessons, you must immerse yourself in a new or challenging situation and see it as an opportunity for learning and growth. Second, you must stay curious and willing to experiment if you want to gain new insights. Third, you need to internalize what you learn by seeking feedback and taking time to reflect. Lastly, you must use these experiences as you adapt to new circumstances and discover what works and what does not. Eventually, you develop what's known as unconscious competence.

To truly develop this capacity, you must also forget the idea that you already know everything. Lessons constantly find their way to us, as long as we maintain an open, learning mindset.[14] Possessing a growth mindset is essential if you wish to achieve learning agility. It helps you see what you have the potential to accomplish, especially when you face challenges. It allows you to navigate difficult situations, to flourish in new environments, and to let go of the "old" to see the "new" space with fresh eyes.

In Wisconsin, I had to learn many things and needed to immerse myself in the process of learning in order to uncover them. Sadly, many leaders do not openly talk about the challenging times or the lessons they learn during them. I believe it would be a great benefit if they did, especially from the standpoint of becoming a mentor and reflecting on their own leadership development.

---

13 Marilyn Wood Daudelin, "Learning from Experience through Reflection," *Organizational Dynamics* 24, no. 3 (Winter 1996): 36–48, https://doi.org/10.1016/S0090-2616(96)90004-2.

14 Angela M. Passarelli and David A. Kolb, "The Learning Way: Learning from Experience as the Path to Lifelong Learning and Development," in *The Oxford Handbook of Lifelong Learning*, ed. Manuel London (New York: Oxford University Press, 2020), 97–129, https://doi.org/10.1093/oxfordhb/9780197506707.013.6.

As a mentor, you have an opportunity to shepherd others through their own moments of learning and discovery, in the hopes that they become better versions of themselves. To do so, it helps if you are willing to share stories of your own journey, including insights into the steps you took to overcome challenging moments. Sharing such insights with others can encourage them to take on growth roles and develop their own self-knowledge that will lead to future success.

Understanding your personal history can help you identify beliefs or patterns that might explain why you care about certain issues or circumstances. Critical lessons from the past help generate insightful roadmaps for leadership space you can explore. My personal and professional life experiences have contributed to my learning agility, and the way I exert my leadership. I was born in the Congo (DRC), grew up there and in Belgium, emigrated to Canada, and then finally settled in the United States.

To date, I have been fortunate to have lived and worked on almost every continent. Every stop has taught me the importance of learning and adapting. Many experiences in different companies, across a range of markets and global teams, have helped me sharpen my learning agility in the business world. As I have learned new competencies, I have also unlearned others and continued to adapt my thinking whenever the context has changed.

I believe that what we learn in challenging situations can pay dividends in the moment and even larger payoffs down the road. In Wisconsin, I had every reason to quit. I did not. Staying helped me expand and grow my skills. In the midst of my experience, we indeed needed to leverage our technology in order to go into new markets and accomplish the CEO's objectives.

Once my skills and knowledge were up to speed and I'd internalized their priorities, I proposed to the CEO that building from our core technology competencies was the key to supporting a much larger cross-functional group focus. To succeed, I explained, we should know with clarity what we were good at and what competencies we needed to develop in order to capture future growth opportunities. The CEO provided me with all the resources I needed and introduced this program in front of all employees.

Looking back, I'm reminded of something that a mentor told me years ago: when you are in one place, your mind must not be in two places. When I first met the CEO, and for the next few weeks, my mind was in two places—to stay or to quit. I chose to stay and found ways to make the most of it. My tenacity in extracting something worthwhile from this experience and my determination to succeed earned his respect.

By the end of my time in Wisconsin, I discovered that sometimes the person you must truly empower is yourself, even when you are focused on helping to empower others. I have no doubt that you have found yourself in your own version of this situation. Perhaps a senior leader made your work life miserable or you were at a loss as to where you could find support. If such a situation is already in your rearview mirror, don't be afraid to look back and see what you learned.

Perhaps there is a story or lesson you can leverage and share with others to support their journeys. Maybe you developed a critical skill that you still lean on today. Whatever the case, I believe that when we learn to thrive in challenging environments, it provides a type of personal fortitude we can leverage later. In the book *The Reflective Practitioner*, the author suggests experiences must be accompanied by reflection.[15]

In the story above, mental agility found its way forward as I sought ways to expand my knowledge and gain new skills. Meanwhile, learning agility showed up as I took things I had previously learned or experienced and applied them to new and different scenarios. People agility (the ability to connect with others on an emotional level) arrived through making connections with new team members and colleagues. Olaf, for instance, was happy to help me succeed.

At the same time, the CEO eventually became an unexpected ally. Finally, change and results agility came about because I was flexible, adapted to uncertainty, and evolved my understanding of the context around me. I remained curious and continued to learn and seek new ways to deliver. I also expressed a range of emotions during this experience, including self-awareness, which allowed me to know when to take stock of situations and how to respond. Equally important, I learned with clarity what type of environments I truly thrive in.

Here is one more note about this story. In the end, what the CEO was hoping to achieve—reversing the profitability loss—did not materialize for US units. As a company, we did not deliver on his bet. Eventually, the board of directors dismissed all of us in the senior team and merged our division with another. We had heard the rumors and saw it coming for weeks, so none of us were surprised when it happened.

---

15 Donald A. Schön, *The Reflective Practitioner: How Professionals Think in Action* (Oxfordshire, UK: Routledge, 2017).

LET US GET STARTED

We don't always have everything we need to succeed. By embracing learning agility, we can draw from lessons and experiences to face uncertainty and meet challenges that come our way. Learning agility is defined as "the willingness and ability to learn new competencies in order to perform under first-time, tough, or different conditions."[16] Learning agility allows a person to adapt to change and grow stronger in the process. I recommend the following actions to help you enhance your competence in your practice and pursuit of embracing experience and agility:

1. **Reflect on pivotal moments in your life and career.** Take yourself on a journey of self-exploration. Reflect on pivotal moments of your life, personal and professional. Draw a timeline and mark what you would consider the highs and the lows. Reflect on why some were considered highs and others lows and how both types impacted you. For each pivotal moment, what did you learn? What was necessary for you to unlearn?

2. **Engage in self-observation and reflection.** Keep a journal and ask reflective questions to extract insights from what is driving your behavior. Did you hear anything new today or something that challenged your past belief? In time, look at patterns of your reflections. This practice gives you an opportunity to not only be present, but also improve your self-awareness.

---

16   Michael M. Lombardo and Robert W. Eichinger, "High Potentials as High Learners," Human Resource Management 39, no. 4 (2000): 321–329, https://doi. org/10.1002/1099-050X(200024)39:4<321::AID-HRM4>3.0.CO;2-1.

Chapter 4

SEEK POSITIVE DISRUPTION

Being a leader of significance is not about maintaining the status quo or doing what everybody else is doing. No one can achieve their personal best by keeping the status quo. From your position, you can encourage others to venture beyond the current norms and explore new options. Of course, in the process, you must be willing to do the same. This is key for making things happen.

In chapters 4 and 5, I'd like to return to the one aspect of transformation that took place during my time in India, the story I shared in the introduction, starting with seeking a way to create a positive disruption.

SAYING YES TO SOMETHING NEW

You do not always know when or where an opportunity for making an impact will come. This was the case for me when

I answered the phone and said hello to a recruiter from Korn Ferry. "I have an opportunity in India for you," he said. "It's with a large regional player in the paints and coatings industry. They're looking for someone to help their research and development organization, mainly to put best practices into place. They also want this person to help with innovation."

"India?" I replied. "I'm not sure. It's very far away." At that point, I had been looking into opportunities elsewhere in Asia, primarily in China. Still, I agreed to at least consider the position and asked to see the description. As I read it, I became more and more intrigued. However, when I tried to delve deeper, I couldn't find much information about the company. "What are they all about?" I wondered. They did not have any publication, nor did they show up on conference lists.

A few days later, I reconnected with the recruiter. I was curious to know why the company was looking for a foreigner to fill the position. "All I know is they haven't been able to fill it locally," he said. "They'd like to bring in someone from overseas who could bring a new level of best practices into the fold."

I decided to fly to India and meet with company executives. Everyone was extremely polite and cordial, but I noticed that people at different levels worked in siloed ways. The same was true in common areas. For instance, managers ate alone in their offices, while their direct reports ate in small groups in the company cafeteria. There was very little intermingling and all the doors up and down every hallway were closed. Perhaps what they needed more than anything was fresh air.

CHALLENGE THE PROCESS

By nature, I was very comfortable introducing myself to everyone I encountered. I began to do this during my initial visit and made it a daily practice in my first few weeks with the company. Taking on a new job is an ideal opportunity to ask probing questions, as many people are happy to get to know the new person.

I discovered that the business environment was rather hierarchical—all reporting needed to go up the chain. Internally, the most significant pressures for change came from administrative processes, which were riddled with inefficiencies. I also found that once various steps within projects moved up the chain, they would bottleneck. Team members would get sidelined as they waited for approval.

What's more, there was a lack of collaboration, which did not surprise me, considering the silos I encountered early on. This exacerbated the frustration that people, especially eager employees, were already feeling. They were doing their work, but managers were stalling whenever they had to review or approve various processes. In turn, this put projects on hold that otherwise would be moving quite seamlessly. The company would never achieve greatness unless they were willing to change their business-as-usual attitude.

Intellectually, employees understood the need for change. However, they had been operating in this fashion for so long that the idea of change was daunting. The organization had invested heavily in their own status quo. Any change would come with varying levels of resistance.

I decided to appoint a group of employees, bright scientists and young managers filled with passion to look for ways to work differently and to get things done, to challenge the status quo. I instructed them to focus their attention less on routine operations and more on what had not been tested before. Their task was to systematically examine our workings, identify bottlenecks and duplications, and make suggestions. They were to identify and remove self-imposed constraints and organizational dogmas. I was expecting them to go with a hardy attitude about the change. "I don't want to hear that we have done it this way," I told them. I initiated a similar challenge when I was working in North Carolina, and the results were impactful.

Here, the team came back and had numerous proposals, including the creation of platforms, aligning some groups with existing businesses, and leveraging expertise around projects. They also proposed the contours of an organization, and I asked them to present it to the whole organization. They shared the issues and problems and opportunities.

I liked many of their ideas and helped team members refine some of them. During a meeting, I explained how we would begin to organize ourselves around projects and create project teams to implement and drive them forward. These teams would follow a horizontal management structure, rather than strictly vertical. We would benefit from agility and avoid bottlenecks in the process.

"This means that if you have been reporting to a specific manager in the past, now you will be part of a project team because you have the skills to accomplish these tasks," I said. "It is time to bring your skills into the light of day—for your own development and also for the sake of the company." In sharing this, I recognized that these changes would affect members of the team. I saw a bit of apprehension on a few faces. "I understand that these new processes and structures are coming with their own set of issues," I said. "Don't worry; we will manage them together."

I was excited because we were able to disrupt by tapping into the passions of different employees as well as their collective spirit of innovation. This approach also lessened the forces involved in the status quo and reduced resistance from most employees. As they were exposed to problems and opportunities, they uncovered solutions. I took the idea of leveraging expertise and forced the transfer of some people across groups and projects.

Along the way, there was indeed resistance from some managers. They felt this new way of working would be too disruptive to their groups and did not want to share resources. My view then was the same as now: you must honor the feelings of and feedback from those who resist. Doing so builds more synergy, shows people that you hear them, and, in many cases, wins new allies.

We addressed many concerns through education and communication, and even called on some reluctant managers to participate in implementing the change. As we went forward with the change, we continued to hold meetings and organized a series of town hall meetings to review and address employee concerns. Overall, we wanted to ensure that as many people as possible knew that the changes we were implementing were focused on the highest priorities. We also made sure to brief the heads of various business units in order to gain their support.

The company soon saw an uptick in output among groups

that were working in this new, collaborative way. In addition, employees who participated in these new teams reported being happier than they had been before. In fact, as days and weeks went on, more and more employees began to flood my office, asking for a chance to be part of the project groups. Everyone was eager to extend themselves in new ways.

At the same time, I knew this was just a start and that more collaboration and learning was right around the corner. This change opened the door to a collaborative environment, which led to the development of new products. Within our first year, seven new products, each of which had been bottlenecked in the pipeline, made their way to commercialization. This was evidence of a very large spike in productivity.

OPENING DOORS

Despite this new energy, many doors remained closed. Managers, senior leaders, nearly everyone with a door kept theirs closed to anyone who may be passing through the hallways. It made me think of my old colleague Jim from Ohio. Would he have knocked on my door all those years earlier had it been closed?

When leaders keep their doors closed, the message is clear: "Don't bother me; my time is more valuable than yours." This will never support the dynamics of a group or encourage an environment that cherishes innovation or creativity.

It can take a long time to build trust in an organization, especially one in which inertia has set in or where change has been slow to come by. It can take months, even years, before people fully trust that you have their best interests at heart, that you want to listen to them, or that you value their input and ideas. As small as it may seem, an open door is a sign of empathy and an invitation to add your ideas to a larger pool of thinking and considerations.

Now, this doesn't mean that you will agree with everything someone says or shares, or that you have to be passive in your conversation. On the contrary. But it does mean that you are expressing a willingness and desire to listen. It says you are ready to hear and to find out how they feel about certain topics, work related or otherwise.

REFLECTIONS

Taking on a new role at a company is an opportunity to ask probing questions and challenge the way things are being done. In fact, this is expected of you. Consider asking questions like "Why are we doing it this way?" or "How might we do this better?"

Challenging the status quo is an opportunity for you to do your best and to bring a dose of energy into the organization.[17] It is a journey into untested waters that might push your competence and force you to draw upon skills that you did not know you possess.

As a leader of significance, you need to stand out in front at times such as these—to be motivated by the sense of discover-

---

17   Michael J. Grant and Thomas S. Bateman, "Charismatic Leadership Viewed from Above: The Impact of Proactive Personality," *Journal of Organizational Behavior* 21, no. 1 (2000): 63–75, http://dx.doi. org/10.1002/(SICI)1099-1379(200002)21:13.3.CO;2-A.

ing what is possible while dipping your toes into new waters. Your focus must be on removing organizational constraints that inhibit creativity and innovation.

Seize the opportunity to improve, make things happen, and tap into employee's passion. Research shows that when asked how things could be different, employees generally imagine how they could be better, not worse.[18] Other research indicates that being proactive produces better results than being reactive.[19]

As you go forward, there will be stakeholders who will provide support for the type of change you wish to install. Seek them out. Their involvement will give them a sense of achievement and satisfaction, especially as changes begin to happen. Having them in your corner can help you drive even more radical change later.

Very few companies are ready to make change, and many respond to change in a haphazard, unplanned fashion. Generally speaking, only a handful of senior managers out there actually want to change anything.[20] They are quite content with the way things are. As a leader of significance, you know that doing better means challenging the current way in which things happen. Some changes will be big, others small. Regardless of the size, every change is about opening new possibilities.

---

18   Adam Mastroianni and Ethan Ludwin-Peery, "Things Could Be Better," PsyArXiv, November 15, 2022, https://doi.org/10.31234/osf.io/2uxwk.

19   Scott E. Seibert and Maria L. Braimer, "What Do Proactive People Do? A Longitudinal Model Linking Proactive Personality and Career Success," Personnel Psychology 54, no. 4 (2001): 845–875, http://dx.doi.org/10.1111/j.1744-6570.2001.tb00234.x.

20   Jeffrey D. Ford and Laurie W. Ford, "Decoding Resistance to Change," Harvard Business Review, April 2009, https://hbr.org/2009/04/decoding-resistance-to-change.

Leadership of significance is about taking initiative in order to make a difference. It has been my experience that when you make something happen, you bring new energy into a system. In the end, it does not matter whether you find the challenge or whether the challenge finds you.

How can you engage your team members and harness their energies in ways that will give rise to new ways of thinking? To do so, you must create a sense of psychological safety where employees feel confident to speak up about important issues, beginning with ways in which you engage and connect with others.[21] The feeling of connection that you create leads to greater commitment, giving employees room to flourish.[22] Such connections can become first steps toward creating something much more transformative: an atmosphere where the people who report to you are the ones who become leaders.

The transformation I embarked on in India created a great deal of energy and liberated the pent-up passion that many employees felt. The ensuing collaboration led to even more energy throughout the organization. The first spark of energy may have come from building new collaborations, but the collaborations themselves set off a chain of events that literally opened the doors that initially remained closed.

You see, cross-department and group collaborations got people out of their silos. They were walking back and forth, jaunting

---

21   Jennifer J. Kish-Gephart et al., "Silenced by Fear: The Nature, Sources, and Consequences of Fear at Work," *Research in Organizational Behavior* 29 (2009): 163–193, http://dx.doi.org/10.1016/j.riob.2009.07.002.

22   Richard H. Thaler and Cass R. Sunstein, *Nudge: Improving Decisions about Health, Wealth, and Happiness* (New York: Penguin Books, 2009).

from this work area to that, and talking all of the time. The hallways began to buzz with project-focused conversations, which also spilled over into the cafeteria and common areas. Leveraging that passion and the spirit of innovation helped achieve the positive disruption we were seeking.

Change is never easy. It takes energy to be excited by change. The response of your followers, individually and collectively, is what will shape the culture of the organization into the future. These first steps were merely the beginning of what became a seismic shift for the company. Chapter 5 continues this story, starting with the next small step in a much larger transformation.

LET US GET STARTED

We can agree that innovation is important and that trying new approaches can result in unexpected, even exciting outcomes. When you disrupt the status quo in a constructive way, you enable adaptation, learning, creativity, and growth.[23] However, change can be scary for many people because of what's known as status quo bias.[24]

The status quo is a safety zone. To disrupt it, you must be willing to step beyond it. As a leader of significance, I encourage you to be bold and brave. At the same time, honor those who resist—they, too, bring value to your endeavors. Here are a few

---

23 Robert M. Davison, "The Transformative Potential of Disruptions: A Viewpoint," *International Journal of Information Management* 55, no. 2 (2020): 102149, http://dx.doi.org/10.1016/j.ijinfomgt.2020.102149.

24 Brittany Harker Martin, "Unsticking the Status Quo: Strategic Framing Effects on Managerial Mindset, Status Quo Bias and Systematic Resistance to Change," *Management Research Review* 40, no. 2 (2017): 122–141, http://dx.doi.org/10.1108/MRR-08-2015-0183.

actions that can help you strengthen your competence in the practice of seeking positive disruption:

1. **Proactively identify opportunities** to create a paradigm shift for the benefit of organizational stakeholders. Generate provocative conversations that evoke deep questioning. Start by asking "Why?" Lead conversations about key mindsets that need to be disrupted and operational improvement opportunities. Intentionally break the organizational routines and habits to allow for space for new thoughts. Encourage people to be more imaginative and seek different ways of thinking; venture outside job descriptions and explore beyond current organizational constraints.

2. **Take risks.** Break problems into small, doable steps. Sometimes a small step can nurture experimental attitudes. Test, then retest, your ideas. Create an environment where employees feel safe. Fear prevents people from venturing beyond their comfort zone and blocks the free exchange of information. Reject the idea that "failure is not an option" as well as the need to "be right the first time." These are paralyzing concepts and can keep people from experimenting or trying new things.

Chapter 5

INSPIRE A SHARED VISION

Employees expect leaders to be forward looking. They expect leaders to talk about not only what is today, but also what can be. So, as a leader of significance, you need to be able to articulate exciting future possibilities and give the work being done a sense of purpose. This is a competency of a leader. Imagine the future for yourself and others. It is not just about your vision, but also about a shared vision.

To develop the capacity to envision the future, you need to spend time in the future. In Chapter 5, I'll continue the story from Chapter 4, starting with the importance of inspiring a shared vision.

GETTING THE MESSAGE

As I was watching TV, I heard an environmental activist accusing paint companies of poisoning children with lead in their formulations. I was shocked at the fact that most paints in Southeast Asia still contained lead and kept wondering why we could not remove it from paints in this part of the world. "The answer is simple," a colleague said to me. "We only need to comply with government regulations, and governments over here do not regulate the use of lead."

I have been sensitive to environmental issues for a very long time. I'm no activist, but throughout my career, I have been concerned about the environmental impact of the chemicals that my industry uses so regularly in various product formulations. Plenty of companies are happy to "be compliant" with government regulations, but very few take additional steps on their own toward transformation or creating lasting change. I wanted companies to think beyond compliance and find ways to shift portfolios toward a greener future—starting with the company I was working for.

This idea continued to germinate in my head during my first six months in India. As I continued to read more about laws and regulations in this part of the world and the technical approaches the industry in Western countries was devising, something hit me. I could not possibly continue to tread on the same path of compliance, realizing the health dangers of some of the compounds we were using.

I continued to travel throughout the marketplace to meet customers and get their perspective on our company, especially where the notion of innovation was concerned. Very few customers actually saw us as an innovative firm. Instead, they recognized our extensive product portfolio. We had won a sizable market share but hadn't won people over on account of our creativity or imagination.

Back at our headquarters, I started having conversations with peers and colleagues about environmental and health issues. No one saw these as major concerns. I felt differently. I believed that our industry could do better and that our company could lead the way in our part of the world.

Soon I began to form a thesis—not a plan, but an idea about what was happening or, more precisely, what wasn't happening. The chairman and I met regularly, and he encouraged me to think of our company as one that competes on the global stage. What I saw was something different: a company that was entrenched in regional business, succeeding in our small, confined space.

I shared my thesis with the energized team members from among the collaborative groups that had continued to form. One day I asked them rather overtly, "Instead of being compliant, what would happen if we sought something more inspirational? What if we became a sustainable operation that used fewer harmful materials and strived to not harm the environment? What if we actually used indigenous, organic materials, while still creating quality products?"

SHARING THE WORK OF A VISION

I began my crusade by sharing a question: What would be the implications of this possible future for the company and society? This opened up conversations. As I kept talking to more people and doing my own research, the vision of this potential future slowly began to emerge and capture more imaginations.

During this time, I attended the first Industrial Green Chemistry Workshop and saw a keynote by Dr. Warner of the Warner Babcock Institute for Green Chemistry. I was intrigued by his presentation as he articulated the incredible business opportunities that could be realized by developing and using safe materials.

When I returned to the office, I shared my excitement and told my enthusiastic employees that we needed to have the foresight and vision to start practicing green chemistry. Not long after, our firm sent five technical professionals to visit Dr. Warner's lab, where they could learn more about green chemistry and gain a better sense of how a move toward green solutions could help our business and potentially lead our industry forward.

A leader's vision requires a significant amount of support to be brought to fruition. Without adequate backing, the vision may stall. Early in my career, when I was still new to managing, my goal was to get to know people within the org and to lead in a way that aligned with their dreams as much as possible. Some fifteen years later, across the other side of the globe in India, I was still driven to do the same thing. With a decade and a half of leadership experience by then, I knew that this approach was the key to helping the company succeed.

Many creative talents were lurking just below the surface, waiting to rise to the top. It was easy to see that the company was filled with untapped energy, especially among the budding group of younger, eager employees. Something was there, but they did not know how to express it. There were too many layers to battle through in order to make their voices heard. I needed to bring them along.

Clear, consistent, and enthusiastic communication was also key. As more technical people learned about the idea of sustainable materials, some began researching related topics, while others voiced concerns, admitting that they weren't sure if applying a sustainable approach to paints and coatings was worth the effort.

Taking all of their feedback into consideration, I gathered a small group together to discuss the merits of my inquiry. Eventually, I gained the support of a critical mass of employees. House paints alone use a great deal of petroleum-based compounds. When consumers are finished with paints, they generally ship them off to landfills. I challenged employees to look for ways in which we could turn all of this around. In the process, the business case for sustainability became more and more compelling.

As they jumped into their own pieces of the vision, I dove deeper into what was happening globally in the paints and coatings industry. Throughout North America and most of Europe, the big push to build a green portfolio was underway. It was only a matter of time before this same emphasis came to the Asian market. Considering the CEO's desire to compete globally, I saw no reason to wait. Plus, on a personal level, I knew that it was better for the planet to make a turn toward a greener way of doing business.

The deeper I studied, the more opportunities I found. Now a new question arose: Were we willing and ready to invest in developing our own green portfolio? I met with my team and discussed the steps we needed to take before we could communicate the vision that was forming. "This could be the company's next iteration," I said. "It will open up an entirely new level of opportunities and potential, as long as we can galvanize our enthusiasm with members of leadership."

MAKING THE VISION COME TO LIFE

I could see in my mind various representations of how my vision of the future might play out in the real world. For example, customers would no longer need to wait a day or two before they entered into newly painted rooms or be afraid of painting their nurseries, worried about harmful chemicals in the air. As I described these ideas to my team, I also explained how each of them could contribute their expertise to bring this future forward. I wanted them to understand their roles so they could see why these changes were necessary and how they would affect the world on a person-to-person level.

Soon enough, team members began to share their own ideas of what was possible. They brought new ways to contribute to the table and shared articles and other online resources we could study and leverage. At this moment I realized that they, too, were internalizing the vision to the point where it was now a shared vision.

With a great deal of excitement and enthusiasm building among our group, I tasked them with the next steps: to help me define and communicate the vision in such a way that would inspire the entire company to follow.

REFLECTIONS

Where does a vision come from? As a process, it is difficult to describe. It comes from what you care deeply about, something bigger than yourself. At first, it can be more of a feeling or a gut sense that comes from concerns, desires, and hopes. Then, slowly, you discover themes that tie together the various whispers in your head. Soon the vision becomes a projection of your inner sense, be it about technology, people, economics, or another broad topic that compels you to wonder. More than anything, a vision takes you on a journey of self-exploration and creation.

In the end, a vision is the synthesis of many things, filtered through the lens of who we are and what we really care about. We all have access to similar information, but some of us are only concerned with executing the task at hand. In today's competitive world, this mindset will not produce extraordinary results. A vision blends instincts, hunches, data, and intellect, pointing the way through and beyond the places others have failed to traverse.

One of your roles as a leader of significance is to be a storyteller, a dream weaver, and a person who can inspire sustained motivation and creativity while you and others march toward the vision. In fact, articulating a vision can create a lasting sense of purpose that propels the work people must do.[25]

In your journey as a leader, you have acquired a great deal of knowledge and information, all of which you can draw on in

---

25 Catherine Bailey and Adrian Madden, "What Makes Work Meaningful—or Meaningless," *MIT Sloan Management Review* 67, no. 1 (Summer 2016): 52–61, https://sloanreview.mit.edu/article/what-makes-work-meaningful-or-meaningless/.

order to solve problems. In addition, somewhere in your subconscious, you have also incorporated your instincts, which lift you up from the crowd. If a vision gives you direction and purpose, pursuing it must also give you energy.

The process of envisioning the future starts with a sense that something big needs to happen or something major must change. Things can be fuzzy at the start, even if you believe in the act of improving the present.

In a way, following a vision is an iterative process. As you move toward it, things become clearer in increments. At some point, you arrive at something that you and others can see and express. As you eventually see the end and share the idea with others, you begin to see how their aspirations can merge with your vision, especially when they want to be part of the future you are foretelling.

What is out there for you right now? Have you maximized your discoveries? Or have you only accumulated your knowledge and comfortably remained within the old tracks?

When you strike forth toward a vision, you will challenge business as usual. You will also provide the context in which something new can emerge. When you step forward, it clarifies for others that it is possible to step into the unknown. But you must be willing to go there first.

Once you do, and you lead others into this place, you must invest time and energy toward giving them the support they need to maintain their own confidence. It's easy to get lost in the unknown, especially if you cannot connect the dots between the small steps and the bigger idea. Therefore, no matter how large or grand a vision is, don't overlook the details that will eventually take you there.

When you share your vision, it must become a shared vision if you want others to care. You must enlist them in a way that appeals to their aspirations. Sharing your vision as a leader is not enough if you truly want to rally people around your idea. They will not follow you into the unknown if there is nothing for them on the other side. Similarly, once in the unknown, they may back out if they feel like they have no say or input into what happens next. They must see themselves as being part of the vision as it comes into form.

When you truly understand and take to heart the hopes and dreams of others, you breathe life into the idea of a shared vision and forge a unity of purpose. You show others that this vision is for the common good. With enthusiasm, you draw a picture of what that future could be. You create images of the future to make it real and vivid. Research shows that our memories recall images better than words.[26]

As a leader, you can be sure that every employee is dreaming of a better tomorrow, but they may not know how to articulate it. At the same time, they also want to see meaning in what they are doing right now, regardless of what tomorrow brings.[27] When a vision is shared, it elevates the human spirit and creates space

26   Rachel Gillett, "Why We're More Likely to Remember Content with Images," *Fast Company*, September 18, 2014, https://www.fastcompany.com/3035856/ why-were-more-likely-to-remember-content-with-images-and-video-infogr.

27   Parker J. Palmer, *Let Your Life Speak: Listening for the Voice of Vocation* (Hoboken: John Wiley & Sons, 2015).

for employees to release their own visions. This helps them move beyond the morass of now and toward something greater.

Developing a shared vision is a cooperative effort of co-creation.[28] Inviting others to participate builds action for change and allows them to find harmony with one other.[29] This happens from interactions with employees and aligns with their aspirations. As a leader, you make them feel as if they can achieve something big. This approach increases their level of commitment and engagement.[30] In turn, they constitute a community of change agents and recruit others to espouse the same vision.[31]

What is your vision? What future do you hope to build? We generally do not take time for soul-searching in a way that actually helps us find clues for a different future. When we finally connect with our instincts, we must act on them. One important lesson I learned over the years is that you must constantly communicate your vision. The more you communicate, the more it resonates with others.

Speak authentically about your convictions. Doing so makes others proud of working for your organization and being part of

28 Robert D. Benford and David A. Snow, "Framing Processes and Social Movements: An Overview and Assessment," *Annual Review of Sociology* 26, no. 1 (2000): 611–639, http://dx.doi.org/10.1146/annurev. soc.26.1.611.

29 Timothy Kuhn, "A Communicative Theory of the Firm: Developing an Alternative Perspective on Intra-organizational Power and Stakeholder Relationships," *Organization Studies* 29, nos. 8–9 (2008): 1227–1254, https://doi:10.1177/0170840608094778.

30 Jesse Newton and Josh Davis, "Three Secrets of Organizational Success," *strategy+business*, July 14, 2014, https://www.strategy-business.com/article/00271.

31 Fred Luthans, "The Need for and Meaning of Positive Organizational Behavior," *Journal of Organizational Behavior* 23, no. 6 (2002): 695–706, https://doi:10.1002/job.165.

something big. As we discussed earlier in the book, this shows them that you are a person on a mission and draws people toward you like emotional contagion.

What can you do in your current space? Where can you find the early wins? What is holding your company back? Who wants to step up to achieve something new? With questions like these in mind, ask yourself: How can I arrive at a vision? Envisioning the future starts with a sense that something needs to happen, and whatever it is, it is worth doing.

When you know what trends and boundaries exist in your industry, you can challenge others to think beyond these limitations. Providing a new perspective will help you stand out. Keep in mind that some may disagree with you. But as a leader of significance, you must challenge the status quo and strike forth on your vision. How else will the future happen?

LET US GET STARTED

The dream of a future you would like to create comes from deep inside—a mix of intuition, study, conversations, and even whispers that occur within you. If you can tune in to them, you can create a vision so big it will require the help of others to achieve it.[32]

Engaging with others enriches a vision and makes it a shared experience.[33] People will follow once they can also embrace a vision as their own. They will get excited when they believe

---

32 Bailey and Madden, "What Makes Work Meaningful."

33 Parker J. Palmer, *Let Your Life Speak: Listening for the Voice of Vocation* (San Francisco: Jossey-Bass, 2000).

they are doing something that will make a big difference in the lives of others. When you help employees connect with purpose, it leads to high levels of engagement, productivity, enthusiasm, and trust.[34] I recommend the following actions to help you strengthen your competence in the practice of inspiring a shared vision:

1. **Search for what is out there.** You have to stop, look, and listen. Take time off from your calendar and your devices, and give yourself space to think, dream, reflect, and listen. Make note of what people are saying in the news and in the marketplace. What trends are percolating? What driving forces are coming to the surface? What would happen if various forces were to collide? Talk to customers and others outside your company.

2. **Listen to people around you.** What do they think should change in your company or industry? Listen to the weak signals as well as the strong ones. What are they telling you? Listen to the whispers inside you as well as the instincts that urge you in one particular direction or another.

3. **Enroll others in your vision.** Start conversations with colleagues about their own dreams, passions, and aspirations. Doing so will help you extend your vision. Discuss where your vision and theirs overlap. Get them excited about what you see. Your vision must entice them. Start the conversation with open-ended questions. Ask "What if?" This will help you identify places where visions and ideas align. Express the future you want to see happen and get them as excited as you are. Think big, but strive for simplicity and pragmatism.

---

34   Susan Price. "A New Study Reveals Which Employees Really Have Purpose and Why You Want to Hire Them," *Forbes*, June 10, 2016, https://www.forbes.com/sites/susanprice/2016/01/10/a-new-study-reveals-which-employees-really-have-purpose-and-why-you-want-to-hire-them/?sh=7c0acead65b7.

Chapter 6

ENGAGE WITH YOUR TEAMS

If you want to inspire and motivate others to enact your vision, you have to start by creating a personal relationship with members of your team. You have to establish that emotional connection with them. Chapter 6 is about how trusted relationships can fuel engagement—and how engagement fuels trust.

The emotions you give to others will ignite their passion. What you discover is that when employees trust their leader, they will more likely engage in a leader's vision and apply their minds and hearts to bring the vision to fruition. Similarly, if you want that level of performance that comes from trust, then you must also demonstrate that you trust your followers before asking for their trust.

GETTING TO KNOW EVERYONE

As I have shared throughout this book, when I'm new to a company, I make a point of speaking with as many people as I can, especially those within my organization. In the process, I offer more than just a handshake. I am most interested in asking questions and getting to know people I will work closely with, mentor, and lead.

Since I am curious by nature, this type of engagement comes relatively easy for me. I have noticed that these types of interactions pay large dividends for the organization as well. For one, they help to build bridges between management and employees. They also help people build confidence, which in turn inspires them to bring their best, most creative selves to work every day.

When I say "creative," I am speaking in terms of tapping into their innate creative reservoir from where they provide well-thought-out and well-executed solutions, no matter what business challenge the organization faces. Employees crave to be part of something that's big and valuable. When people bring their best ideas and most energetic approaches forward, the company benefits.

There are many things involved in building relationships. Trust is perhaps the most important aspect. Knowing someone well and knowing how they feel and think about a wide range of subjects are the building blocks of trust. As a leader, you must take time to get to know your team members. Go for lunch or spend an evening unwinding in a social setting. As you spend time together, you will get to know your people, and the trust you develop will go both ways.

This will create a space where people feel open to expressing themselves. Some may tell stories about great experiences they have had with certain customers. Others will share new ideas for solving challenges. No matter what people discuss, they will feel comfortable doing so. This type of comfort is another aspect involved in creating psychological safety, which is a key to collaboration and shared ownership.

THE ESSENTIAL NATURE OF COLLABORATION AND TRUST

In product development, collaboration is essential. Yet team members can be possessive and will even look for ways to create solutions in isolation in order to get the credit. When trust is baked into the dynamics of your org, people warm up to each other, look out for one another, and warn other team members about issues, roadblocks, and challenges. They appreciate the expertise around them and openly value each other's contributions and opinions. This paves the way toward greater motivation and mutual feelings of being valued. In such an environment, innovation and experimentation flourish.

At work, as in life, trust creates a loop. On one end of the loop, trust fuels engagement; on the other, engagement inspires more trust. Trust must come from somewhere—but where? I believe it comes from leaders making efforts to understand people at deeper levels than merely saying hello when they pass you in the hallway. It involves consciously wanting to know more about their joys, experiences, and the things that give them energy. People tend to follow someone who knows them, which brings me to a gentleman named Ahmed.

KNOWING THAT YOU BELONG

Ahmed was a graduate from the University of Akron whom I

hired in the early 1990s as a scientist. Right away, it was easy to see how passionate he was about chemistry, and this passion helped to solidify my hiring decision. He was also something of an expert in foaming and antifoaming technologies, which were crucial to our industry.

Ahmed's passion extended throughout every aspect of his work. His eyes lit up when he talked about his job and the technical challenges he tried to solve on a daily basis. On the personal side, Ahmed was a father of three, and being a father was another passion of his. He occasionally brought his children to the office with him and was genuinely excited to show them around, introduce them to colleagues, and explain the work he performed.

One day by the coffee machine, I asked him, "What is it about our place of business that you love? Why do you like working here?" I was expecting that he'd talk about solving challenges or being able to apply his knowledge to complex projects. His reply came from a completely different angle.

"The Ping-Pong table," he said. At first I thought he was joking, and I chuckled a bit. But he was serious. "I really like being able to play Ping-Pong during lunch. It gives me an opportunity to interact with Mike Van Dijk."

Personal motivation can come from any angle. Ahmed was not motivated by money, even though he had a family to take care of. Through the quality of his work, it was clear that he was motivated by what he considered to be his professional purpose: he wanted to apply chemistry in a way that solved complicated challenges. Still, there was another link to his motivation. As I explored it, I saw that playing Ping-Pong was actually a window into something larger: a sense of belonging.

Ahmed saw himself as belonging to something that was bigger than him. He was part of a thoughtful and energetic group within a department that collaborated but also knew how to take time to have a little fun in a supportive way. He had formed a number of bonds with people, many of whom he considered to be good friends. What I came to understand about Ahmed, and have recognized among other employees over my career, is that the notion of belonging to something can be one of the strongest motivators of all.

Employees can take their talents anywhere they like—the world is filled with opportunities for people who want to seek them out. There will always be competition in the workforce, no matter what industry your company is in or the niche in which employees specialize. But the bonds that grow at a company on a person-to-person level can be differentiators. For Ahmed, what he enjoyed most about our workplace was his team, which seemed like a very compelling idea.

The more I sat with this notion, the more it made sense. The desire to be part of a group or collective is embedded deep within human nature. But that doesn't mean we are happy to be a part of just any group. We want to belong to groups that reflect who we are at our core, that invite our participation, and that give us room to be ourselves. I believe that a sense of belonging, far more than mastery, may be the ultimate way to motivate and bring the best out of employees. This idea became a compelling motivation for me as I went about managing this particular group of people.

CREATING PSYCHOLOGICAL SAFETY

The other motivational factor is the notion of psychological safety, which I brought up earlier in this book. Psychological safety goes hand in hand with trust. I remember a story that Maria Teresa Gonzales told me. She would eventually take charge of our product development group. Prior to her working under me, her previous manager had asked her to lead an important project. The first few months went great, and her manager at the time was always seeking her input. "This is a new initiative," he would say, "and I am looking for your ideas."

She really believed that she was working well with this manager. Then things started to change. Maria began to hear from others that her manager was unhappy with her performance. She was surprised about this since she never received negative feedback directly from him. She knew that she could go and ask but didn't have the confidence to do so. Even though the manager continued to encourage her to push the initiative, Maria Teresa noticed that she was no longer being invited to some critical meetings. She began to feel invisible and did not feel a sense of psychological safety that would help her thrive. Eventually, as she sought information, she was ignored or completely shut down. She wanted to leave the company, until I came on board and helped her regain her confidence and trust.

Psychological safety refers to any experience of feeling safe and knowing that others see, hear, and appreciate you. In a safe environment, employees can speak up about their concerns, ask questions, challenge ideas, and take risks. As a leader, being able to inspire engagement starts with creating this feeling of safety, which is a hallmark of trust.

Leadership affects employees' perception of psychological safety. Openness, plus a good relationship between you and employees, will improve their feeling of psychological safety and increase their trust in you as a leader.

Ahmed felt safe enough in that moment to answer my question honestly. He didn't try to hide behind "work-speak," if you will, or give me the type of answer that he thought I might have wanted to hear. Instead, he spoke in a rather off-the-cuff way. When employees feel safe, they seek feedback or even fail without dire consequences. Maria Teresa did not feel safe to approach her previous manager. Eventually, she and I were able to build the type of trust and safety that helped her grow into becoming a very influential leader.

FEELING VALUED

People are always hungry to be seen and to feel valued. Years ago, an employee shared with me how touched he was that I had reached out just to check in because I had not seen him for a while. It was a small but important motivational moment for him. He saw the value in my interaction, even though it was rather small in the grand scheme of business life.

Value comes in many forms. By asking questions and checking in with people, you create a space for them to contribute their thinking. "It's been a while since we've talked..." or "Hello..." may prompt an action. The conversation will go where it goes, but the key is to ask open-ended questions. These simple acts help employees feel seen.

Value comes across in the words you use. Your words matter, as does the way you listen. A VP of human resources once said to me, "At the end of a conversation, both people should feel energized." I like to take this thought even further and add the following: if both people are not energized at the end of a conversation, then it wasn't truly a conversation. There needs to be a mutual feeling of appreciation and motivation for a conversation to resonate.

In conversation with employees, you must find ways to tune in to them and what they're saying. What themes do they share? What is working well for them? What motivates this or that person? How do they prefer to be managed? These things may not come up directly, at least not right away, but over time, they will find their way to the surface naturally.

A leader must also be open during conversations. After all, an open heart is also an open door. Tell them a story and choose themes that engage them on an emotional level. Let them ask questions in return. In fact, encourage them to do so, and answer them when they do. This creates the connection.

This type of two-way communication plants the seed of empathy, where both parties come to know and recognize when the other may need support. Empathy is not about feeling sorry during a bad time or getting pulled into someone else's negativity in an effort to help or fix a situation. Empathy is an action for change.

GIVE A SMALL PUSH

Many years ago I had the pleasure to work with a young engineer named Hilde, who always sat in the back whenever our team met in the conference room. Hilde was very talented, and people often asked her advice and insight into various chemical combinations—she was truly a gifted engineer. Not only that, but she was meticulous in her organizational skills, perhaps one of the most organized people I have ever been around. Our company used petrochemical feedstock as a raw material at the front end of the chemical conversion process.

Every day, Hilde wrote a note for the group about what kind of reaction was running at the plant. She did this on her own, without prompting from her manager, in order to be of service. She clearly was motivated to share insights, but in a quiet way. When I reflected on how she tended to sit in the back of meetings, typically with her arms crossed, I saw it as a posture of defensiveness, even though she wasn't a defensive person. She was confident but quiet.

One day after a group meeting, I asked her to drop by my office. After a moment of checking in, I asked why it was that she chose to stay silent in the background of team meetings. She didn't give much of an answer.

"I know that you understand your work quite well," I said. "People come to you for information, especially related to the feedstock, and we all rely on the list you share every day. You don't have to be intimidated by the other engineers. They might think they're experts, but you are the true expert. They look to you because they know you know. Can you show more of your knowledge when we meet in groups?"

"I can try," she said.

"Great," I replied. "Next week, I'm going to call on you to talk about what's happening with the feedstock in the plant."

Hilde was undaunted and not nervous at all. I even suspected that some part of her had been waiting for me to create this situation. She quickly stepped up and became the de facto expert in all things related to feedstock formulations—not just for our organization, but for the entire company.

Soon everyone in the company began relying on her for the information she had been sharing quietly via her daily list. The best part about it was that she approached this role with great enthusiasm. The focus on her work helped her engage in completely new ways. She had always found value in sharing what she knew, but now the value was looping its way back to her. She actually saw how others valued her for her insights and just how far this value extended across all levels of the proverbial org chart.

In many ways, Hilde's journey reminds me of Jim from Chapter 1. Regardless of talents, some people are simply not inclined to step forward or need a nudge in order to do so. As a leader, creating conditions for people to unleash their potential comes with the territory.

REMEMBER YOUR PERSONAL HISTORY

Hilde's story also reminds me of two things from my own background, long before my professional career. The first comes from high school and my joy for mathematics. My math teacher, for some reason, saw something in me that I did not recognize. He gave me very focused attention as well as the type of encouragement that helped me grow. How?

He called on me, again and again. He did not let me disappear into my notebook or text or sink in my seat. Even if I had not raised my hand—which was often, especially in the beginning of my high school years—he would call on me, hand me the chalk, and send me to the board to figure out an equation in front of the whole class.

The second story comes from a few years later, after I'd earned my bachelor's degree. A professor with whom I'd studied took me to lunch and wanted to know my future plans.

"I don't know," I said. "I suppose I will look for a job."

The professor ran the lab at the school and asked if I'd be interested in working there as I considered my next steps. After we discussed what it would entail, I asked what seemed to be a logical question: "Why me?"

"I have a feeling you'll be good at it," he said. "You have the technical and organizational skills, and also the right personality," he added.

Much like my high school math teacher, my former professor saw something in me that I had not seen. He helped me take a step toward my next endeavor, which did, in fact, pave the way for where I went in my studies and my career.

I share these anecdotes in the hopes of reminding you of how important it is to engage with the people around you, no matter where they are in their professional journeys, and also to reflect on your own journey. As a leader of significance, you must take time to engage with those around you. In the process, you can also re-engage with archived aspects of your own history.

When you do these things, you build the type of trust that encourages employees to bring innovation and commitment to work with them. Employees who feel trusted and seen—and who trust you in return—are prepared to share their innovative ideas. Again, you will have constructed a frame around a place of psychological safety where employees feel they are free to propose ideas, suggest new ways of working, and speak freely, knowing that you are ready to hear them. They see your trust and share the best versions of themselves in response to it.

REFLECTIONS

Is there a secret method or methods for being engaged and thereby building trust? In my experience, the path toward engagement includes two critical pieces: being visible and making time, both of which are connected.

Being visible and making time can be as simple as keeping your office door open—by now you know my opinion of what an open door says to employees. True, we all get busy—there's no denying this fact. Some weeks, you might have to literally carve out time on your schedule for a walkabout or even pencil in an appointment with yourself to make your rounds and say hello. I have had to do these exact things more times than I can count. You have to be visible and mobile; that's how you start to create a circle of trust. People trust those they see.

You have to be visible as well as present. Personal presence is the ability to authentically connect with others. Connect with employees' minds and hearts. When they see the real you, it strengthens the bond of trust. This makes you more approachable and reinforces the connections you are building. As you communicate, you must "communicate richly," to borrow an expression by James Harter and Amy Adkins.[35]

Communication helps build relationships, but it cannot be transactional if you want to engage employees in meaningful ways. Nor can communication be limited to work-related activities. Instead, it must cover ground that goes beyond work. People want deep conversations, and once you realize it, this helps build better relationships.[36]

It takes humility and strength to truly listen to others. As author Stephen Covey wrote, "One must listen with the intent to understand."[37] We journey with them, feel their challenges, and share in their joy. If you believe, as I do, that leadership is about relationships, then listening takes on a whole new meaning.

Neuroscientists tell us that sharing stories increases the neurochemicals that are responsible for compassion, generosity, and empathy.[38] Get to know your employees and create an atmosphere where they feel comfortable to talk about any subject.

There are many opportunities to engage with team members. I have found many points in which leaders can engage and interact with employees: for instance, before or after meetings,

35 James Harter and Amy Adkins, "What Great Managers Do to Engage Employees," *Harvard Business Review*, April 2, 2015, https://hbr.org/2015/04/what-great-managers-do-to-engage-employees.

36 Michael Kardas, Amit Kumar, and Nicholas Epley, "Overly Shallow? Miscalibrated Expectations Create a Barrier to Deeper Conversation," *Journal of Personality and Social Psychology: Attitudes and Social Cognition* 122, no. 3 (2022): 367–398, https://doi.org/10.1037/pspa0000281.

37 Stephen Covey, *The 7 Habits of Highly Effective People* (Free Press, 1988; repr., New York: Simon and Schuster, 2020), 278. Citations refer to the 2020 edition.

38 Gavin J. Fairbairn, "Ethics, Empathy and Storytelling in Professional Development," *Learning in Health and Social Care* 2, no. 3 (March 2002): 2005, 48–55, https://doi:10.1046/j.1473-6861.2002.00004.x.

in the morning as you are filling up your coffee or making tea, while you are getting a snack in the common area, when you are in the parking lot walking to or from the building, and when you are in the reception area or other areas of your workplace where hallways and meeting rooms intersect or where people converge. If you are leading a virtual team or looking for ways to connect with remote workers, you can do this via approved internal social media channels or other software your company uses to connect.

Once you solve the "how" part of creating connections, you'll find that what happens during or within the connection matters much more. Use these moments for impromptu check-ins, and see how your people are doing. For many employees, saying "good morning," or asking "Did you watch the game last night?" is just as meaningful as making formal recognition of something they've accomplished.

Enter conversations with an open mind and a willingness to be surprised by what you are about to hear and learn.[39] During these conversations, ask open-ended questions. When you do, you create space for others to contribute their thoughts. Questions also help convey your interest in their viewpoint. By actively listening, you are doing more than just hearing the words; you are creating a safe space for an engaging conversation.

Ask them, "What do you love about your job? What could be better? What surprised you about this or that particular project?

39 Javier Salas, "Neuroscientist Mariano Sigman: 'Loneliness Is Toxic. Having Someone to Talk to Is Tremendously Important for Our Health,'" El Pais, October 20, 2022, https://english.elpais.com/science-tech/2022-10-20/neuroscientist-mariano-sigman-loneliness-is-toxic-having-someone-to-talk-to-is-tremendously-important-for-our-health.html.

If you had a magic wand, what would you change here?" Then follow up with other questions to elicit critical thinking. In the process, look for ways to stay open to talking about your own aspirations, family, friends, and interests. An open heart is an emotional door. By opening up, you make yourself more vulnerable, which is another key to strengthening trust.[40]

When you begin to engage with team members, you create the basis for future interpersonal interactions. Each engagement builds more and more trust. As I've written, this trust eventually cycles back into the engagement, which supports the company's endeavors.

Initiate these conversations with people at different levels of your company. When you connect with them, you also energize them. In turn, this energy can spark their enthusiasm and passion to see the organization succeed.

Keep in mind that certain managers may be concerned or might wonder what type of conversations you are having with their direct reports. You can quiet these worries by sharing your findings and observations with them.

As you talk to different people, look for overlaps across comments and themes that people share. Perhaps the same thing or topic energizes multiple people. You don't have to come right out and ask about their aspirations, though people may share them organically.

---

40   Steven M. Norman, Bruce J. Avolio, and Fred Luthans, "The Impact of Positivity and Transparency on Trust in Leaders and Their Perceived Effectiveness," *The Leadership Quarterly* 21, no. 3 (2010): 350–364, http://dx.doi.org/10.1016/j.leaqua.2010.03.002.

These types of conversations also allow you to identify potential candidates who have the passion and drive to grow and take on new responsibilities. They also represent an opportunity for you to identify what the authors Zia Khan and Jon R. Katzenbach refer to as "fast zebras" in their book *Leading Outside the Lines*.[41]

Such employees possess the ability to move fast by challenging the formal organization and leveraging informal networks to motivate others. They will be able to help and accelerate the process when you take on large strategic initiatives.

You also must identify employees who have achieved performance in nontraditional ways, be it through technical or business process innovation. These are your potential innovators. If you give them space, you will channel their innovative impulses.

Above all, show empathy. Empathy is not an empty platitude about making people feel better. Rather, it is an action for change and a way to authentically connect with others. Listen to their dilemmas, and see what they need from you. Doing so can help you build sustainable relationships, increase inclusion, and improve engagement and productivity.

Empathy can supercharge activities, make you more approachable, and help establish the fact that you are a person with whom others can share thoughts because they feel safe.

Every word we say matters and carries its own weight. With this in mind, err to the side of motivation and gratitude. After

---

41   Zia Khan and Jon R. Katzenbach, *Leading Outside the Lines* (Hoboken: John Wiley & Sons, 2010).

employees share feedback or insight, ask them, "Can I check if I understand?" or offer a statement of gratitude, such as "Thank you for taking time to share with me." Expressing gratitude is powerful, uplifting, affects employees' well-being, and increases positive emotion. It leaves people feeling good.[42]

The level of interpersonal trust that you bring into these conversations will help to create emotional and psychological safety. Amy Edmondson, a professor at Harvard Business School, has researched this topic quite extensively.[43] You can build psychological safety by creating the right climate and encouraging positive behaviors in your teams.

To do so, you must set the tone for the type of climate you want, thus influencing the team's psychological safety. In other words, you have to model the way. Eventually, this type of engagement will blossom into something else.

LET US GET STARTED

Psychological safety induces the feeling of vitality, which impacts a person's engagement in their work. It is a precursor for greater innovation, improved collaboration and inclusion, and high performance. Supportive leadership brings it to the surface, while an authoritative leadership does the opposite.[44]

---

42 Xuan Zhao and Bertram F. Malle, "Insufficiently Complimentary? Underestimating the Positive Impact of Compliments Creates a Barrier to Expressing Them," *Journal of Personality and Social Psychology* 121, no. 2 (2021): 239–256, https://doi.org/10.1037/pspa0000277.

43 Amy C. Edmondson, *The Fearless Organization: Creating Psychological Safety in the Workplace for Learning, Innovation and Growth* (Hoboken: John Wiley & Sons, 2018).

44 Laura Delizonna, "High Performing Teams Need Psychological Safety. Here's How to Create It," *Harvard Business Review*, August 24, 2017, https://hbr.org/2017/08/high-performing-teams-need-psychological-safety-heres-how-to-create-it.

To strengthen your competence in the practice of engaging with your team, and thereby promote an environment where psychological safety flourishes, I recommend the following actions:

1. **Be visible.** Make yourself visible or easy to find and approach. Move around and find people you haven't seen in a while. You have to be seen if you are going to communicate and know what is going on with employees. Ask powerful questions that send others into a reflective mode about what is important to them and the organization. You can do it in one-on-one or in a team setting, at coffee break, at review meetings, or at company events. Pay attention to what they are doing and what they are feeling.

2. **Get to know others.** Opportunities are everywhere, key junctures where you interact with employees. You will never know employees, who they are and what they are capable of accomplishing, unless you take time to talk to them, at both the personal and professional level. Hold such conversations; this creates more engagement and learning. Use powerful phrases and be generous. Ask questions and seek and invite participation. Repeat these questions because they are powerful. To be trusted, you have to be willing to open up to others. People trust people they know. Share your story.

Chapter 7

ENERGIZE THE ORGANIZATION

As a leader of significance, you have the power to create enlivening moments for employees, teams, and the organization as a whole. You also have the potential to create a strong impact on the level of energy within your organization. Your energy can determine the success of a workday and the overall organization.

By uplifting others through an authentic leadership, you are lifting not only the organization, but also yourself. You want to be the incandescent person that lit up the room. In nature, botanists refer to the "heliotropic effect," which is a phenomenon whereby plants grow in the presence of light.

We are all attracted by this type of life-giving energy. To be an effective leader, you must become what I like to call the "energizer in chief." Being this person will help bring out the best in others, which can energize the entire organization. First, you must cultivate this energy within yourself before you can create it in others. Then, when you do, you will increase the morale, engagement, and performance of those around you. You can energize individuals, teams, and organizations through a wide range of actions, many of which I have shared in Chapter 7.

HELPING OTHERS FLOURISH

While building an organization in India, I had the pleasure of working with a young employee named Lakshman Shah. Lakshman was a very bright young man, but despite his intelligence, he never felt like he could fully materialize his ideas. I saw great potential in him despite his tendency to drift in his thinking or bounce from idea to idea after getting started. Because of his tendency to start and stop, members of management did not really know how to channel his creative energy. In their minds, Lakshman needed a little extra guidance and support to stay focused. For managers and team leaders, this gave them pause whenever they thought about including him on a project. As I said, he was bright and passionate about his work, and I wanted to find a way to help him grow.

One day, Lakshman came to me to tell me about something he was working on: he was trying to create a self-cleaning coating. I could tell right away that he was extremely excited about it—even more excited than usual.

"What excites you most about this project?" I asked.

"To be honest," he began, "there's an international competition and an award associated with it. I think we have something here that would make a pretty strong candidate to go for it. I think we could actually win."

Lakshman was working with a few other people on the project. They joined in for a follow-up meeting and shared a brochure about the contest's parameters. It was indeed a highly competitive contest, and companies such as PPG and Dow had won before. We were nobody in that circle.

Lakshman and his team explained the steps they'd already taken and offered to share the documentation they'd created. They had put a lot of time and effort into their presentation and had a paper and article to go with it. I was on my way to a separate conference, which would require a lot of focus and energy. However, seeing their excitement and thinking that perhaps we did have something worthy here, I told them to share what they had and promised I would take a look at all of it and provide them with prompt feedback.

This single act meant a lot to the group of young employees—they felt valued and seen, and my actions inspired them to dream even bigger and take a chance to shine. It energized them to explore a way to help the company gain recognition, which added to their renewed feelings of belonging.

PUTTING YOURSELF IN A SUPPORT POSITION

I received their material a couple of days later, after I'd arrived at my conference. In between presentations, I took my laptop out and worked on Lakshman's material. It was quite good, and there were only a few places where he and his group needed some additional direction. I continued to respond to everything they sent as quickly and as thoroughly as I could and then would go back to my own work and conference activities.

When I returned from the conference, I did not see Lakshman for a couple of days. Finally, he made a point of stopping by my office.

"Sir," he said. "We sent everything in on time."

"That's excellent news," I said. "I think you have a chance of winning here," I added. "It is a strong concept."

"Now what?" he asked.

"Well," I began, "I suppose you must continue to push on your idea. It has already brought you a great deal of energy. If I understand correctly, it would be a good direction for the company to take. I believe you are just the person to pursue it."

"Will you continue to be involved?" he asked, somewhat reluctantly, as I recall.

"Of course," I said. "It's my pleasure to support the work you're doing."

Lakshman continued to keep me in the loop about his work. Knowing his track record, I was intent to stay with him, yet did not want to push too hard. After all, it was his idea and his project. If I stepped in too intently, it might stifle the energy he was bringing to it naturally.

After a few weeks, I had forgotten all about the contest when Lakshman came bounding down the hallway and into my office. He was almost out of breath.

"Sir, you'll never believe it—we have been selected among the top concepts," he said. "We will need to go to the US for the presentation. Then they will announce the winner."

A few months later, after the presentation in the US, the competition did indeed select Lakshman's concept for the top award, ahead of all other innovative global players. We became the first Indian company ever to win a top international award in coatings technology.

When Lakshman and I met to discuss it, he shared something I was not expecting. "To be honest, we would not have done it without you," he said.

"Without me?" I asked. "You and your team did all of the work. I merely reviewed it and offered some notes."

"Yes, but we knew how busy you were. Still, you continued to be involved. It really meant something to know you were with us on the journey. It helped us maintain our focus and our energy. We did not want to let you down. You helped us keep going."

In their minds, this positive relational energy propelled their performance to a higher level. It nourished them and made them come alive. This energy was also reciprocal, as I, too, became energized.

The ability of a leader to generate relational energy is powerful. In the previous chapter, my point was to show how being and staying engaged is truly a two-way street. You must ask, but you must also give. Here in Chapter 7, the discussion of energy is similar, as creating and sustaining energy is very much the same.

As a leader, you certainly can energize people and teams with enthusiasm and encouragement, but sometimes the greatest and most sustaining way to create energy is to give some of your own, especially when it means giving it to a cause that people care about deeply.

LEARNING FROM STORIES

We have all experienced moments when we recognize the fact that our organizations would benefit from a higher level of energy. This first happened to me while working in North Carolina with the company that needed to complete the technology transfer with its parent Japanese firm.

Stories can be revealing and showcase things that are important to us. I once did an exercise back when I was still in North Carolina. As I had learned by then, the most important work for me to do was to get to know as many people as possible—to learn their strengths, passions, and places where they felt truly energized.

Shortly after starting in North Carolina, I gave employees a chance to introduce themselves with the help of others through their stories. My reason went far beyond breaking the ice or giving people something to talk about. If you want to increase collective motivation, you must strengthen the bonds that your team feels toward one another.

People want to know more about the people they're working

with, and not purely for personal reasons only. People look for skills in others that complement what they bring to the table. They get excited to learn about projects and soon find ways in which they can contribute. These types of connections will put you in position to harness the group's energy via your leadership.

The exercise was actually quite simple: in pairs, employees were to conduct very brief conversational interviews with another person, take notes, and share what they learned. To help frame their conversations, I asked them to ask questions about times when the other person felt most alive at work.

Through this exercise, I tapped into some coursework from my MBA days at Case Western Reserve University, courtesy of my professor David Cooperrider. The work included a focus on organizational DNA and the importance of Appreciative Inquiry. In essence, we looked at the things that actually inspire people and ecological systems to feel most alive.[45] Something else I learned during this time was the importance of stories themselves. They tell you about the storyteller, and they also open up new paths to discovering value.

One story that rose to the surface involved Mr. Li, an older gentleman who had been with the company in North Carolina for many years. Many years prior, we learned during our story-telling exercise, Mr. Li was involved in developing a key process technology for making styrene acrylic emulsions, which was new for the company at the time. Nearly everyone in the room was familiar with some of the products based on this technology. I was even familiar with the process at that point, though still

45   David L. Cooperrider and Diana Whitney, *Appreciative Inquiry: A Positive Revolution in Change* (San Francisco: Berrett-Koehler, 2005).

new to the company. However, none of us actually knew that Mr. Li was the mind behind the process, and our eyes quickly lit up upon hearing his story.

In Mr. Li's younger days, the process associated with solving filtration issues was quite labor intensive. The company had been trying to decrease cycle time and improve productivity in one of their main operation plants using existing filtration systems. People in the plant had been consistently working twelve-hour shifts to find a workable solution, to no avail. They were dealing with exhaustion and desperately needed something to change.

The problem itself did not sound too complicated. It involved the safe and consistent filtration and removal of sediments from the mix. However, nothing the company had tried ever held up—not until Mr. Li's perforated bucket straining breakthrough. This simple solution was an instant success. It improved the filtration rate and was easy to clean. Soon the company implemented the process across all of its facilities. This drastically cut down on filtration time and improved productivity across the board.

For Mr. Li, one of the most enjoyable parts of sharing the story was hearing another employee share it with the group. As the interviewer recalled the story, he talked about the energy Mr. Li exuded as he revisited the experience. Something I found particularly interesting was the fact that Mr. Li had never received recognition for his work. In truth, he was unbothered by the lack of recognition. For him, solving complex problems was always more important than getting an award for doing so.

Another thing we learned from Mr. Li's story was how enlivening the experience had been for him. He already knew that people at the plant trusted him, and this awareness gave him the impulse to do his best. He mentioned that investing time in solving a problem was a big energizer.

As a leader, when you pick up the energy of others, you create new ways to engage and give people new chances to be their best. Mr. Li did not aspire to become a vice president, or even a manager. He was very happy in his position as a senior engineer. What he wanted, however, and what energized him, was to find new ways to contribute to the success of others and to the company as a whole. In that way, his story opened a door that led to a new flow of back-and-forth energy. People entered his sphere in search of support, and he gladly entered theirs to provide it. With new ways to make a difference and see the tangible results of doing so, Mr. Li was energized. Likewise, the team around him improved and grew on account of his energy and enthusiasm.

When you enrich life-giving forces, great things play out. For Mr. Li, the minute he was more engaged, he felt empowered, excited, and at the ready. When he gained recognition for his earlier contribution, it added fuel to an endless cycle—not for the recognition itself, but for the connections it created. In this way, Mr. Li was very similar to Hilde from Chapter 6. Both were diligent, quiet workers who became even more engaged when the chance arrived.

In the end, this exercise of sharing stories went far beyond breaking the ice. It increased collective motivation and helped strengthen the bonds that team members felt. For listeners and witnesses, the stories gave them new ways to connect, empathize, and understand the lives and motivations of their colleagues. Meanwhile, those who shared their stories grew more confident and engaged.

LIFE-GIVING FORCES OF AN ORGANIZATION

When I took the assignment in India trying to build innovation, I quickly saw that the organization could perform at a higher level than it was. Not enough employees were giving their full effort. Even the enthusiastic ones had the tendency to suffer from energy dips, especially when projects were bottlenecked. However, I noticed that they maintained energy when the topic involved fun activities or company events. In fact, in those cases, they did not mind staying late and giving extra time to put things together.

After noticing this a few times, I began to wonder what would happen if my group applied the same amount of energy for work-related activities as when they were prepping for a company gathering. Then I turned the question around a bit and asked myself: What do I need to help generate the same level of energy in our work-related projects?

In relation to the company itself, I was trying to create a sense of community and connection. One of the issues that seemed to be holding the company back was the fact that there was very little collaboration or mutual understanding across and within departments. It was yet another example of people working in silos. This was the same issue that helped trigger the cross-department collaborations I wrote about in Chapter 4. People were so focused on their individual activities that they rarely looked up to find out what others were working on, let alone who the other people were at their core.

One of the HR managers in the learning and development org introduced me to Resonate Consulting. Sushma Sharma, Resonate's CEO, suggested that they could help by taking us on a journey of exploration, which involved a series of Appreciative Inquiry interviews with the whole organization. I was enthusiastic, as I was familiar with the concept. Still, I wasn't certain that we could actually harness new energy, especially given the limited levels of collaboration.

The consultant agreed to work with us to examine the factors that influenced the way our organization functioned. Their goal was to help us maximize our human capital. To do so, they needed to discover the organization through the eyes of each individual in order to understand it as a system. They would help define a baseline of where the organization was in order to prepare the organization to begin achieving a higher level of performance.

The consultants carried out thirty-one interviews across all levels of the organization, including eighteen one-on-one conversations and thirteen focus group discussions across two groups. These were all semi-structured conversations, complete with open-ended questions that allowed room for reflection. The interviews explored moments, events, and stories that illustrated who we were at our best. They provided a sense of discovery about what made things happen around here. They also produced insights into how people felt about their work, their roles, and their place in the company. Quite often in situations like these, feelings are the missing link. Uncovering them can help leaders understand a person's behaviors, actions, and choices to engage or disengage.

When the consultant presented their findings to a group of

senior managers and me, a number of themes began to emerge. As we explored themes, patterns began to reveal themselves. This exercise proved to be quite transformative for the organization. There was a sense of renewed commitment and a release of energy. This work led to the discovery of the life-giving forces that lay buried in the organization.

We could discern, for instance, what it was that gave energy to people, what life-giving forces were present for people before and after they walked into work, what engaged them and truly brought out their best. We also began to explore the negatives: what drained people, what they felt was missing from work, what de-energized them, and the like.

To focus in on themes and patterns, we isolated specific messages, such as the following:

- "My ideas matter, not my position."
- "It is very important that we celebrate our differences."
- "I care about the journey from ideation to privatization."
- "Freedom is essential. I want to be challenged, but I do not want to lose my identity in my pursuit to solve it."
- "It's good to be appreciated and recognized. When I know others see my contributions, it helps me flourish."
- "I care about heart connection. I want to know the people I am working with. I want to know what matters to them and why it matters."

Many life-giving forces of the organization came to the surface in those interviews and the broadened discussion that followed. Among the most outstanding were the following:

- Emotional connection
- Challenges
- Passion to succeed
- Drive for excellence
- Desire to innovate
- Belief in self and others
- Recognition

Some of these life-giving forces were already present in the system. Others came up as things that employees yearned for. The entire exercise was extremely important and revealing. Our conclusion was that people will give their best when they feel most connected to life-giving forces. They will find the missing energy reserves when appreciation, recognition, and personal connections become part of the work taking place.

Organizations tend to focus on problem-solving rather than finding out their life-giving forces as enablers of value creation. The problem-oriented view in organizational practices has several negative impacts on the production of generative knowledge and innovations.

With these revelations at hand, we began creating new levels of engagement with employees and fostering an atmosphere of collaboration and dedication to excellence. The life-giving forces we identified guided and enabled our actions. We knew that creating and maintaining such an environment needed to be our mandate if we were going to truly bring out the best in people and benefit as a company.

REFLECTIONS

We are all capable of building energized relationships. When we do, we bring out the best in others and in ourselves. As leaders, we are the single most important factors that determine how our organizations perform. Our ability to bring new energy to the fore is extremely powerful and of the utmost importance.

Creating energy gives leaders a tremendous advantage. As a leader, you have the power to turn around an organization, starting with revitalizing disengaged employees. When you possess and showcase positive energy, you pave the way for greater engagement, teamwork, and innovation and magnify a sense of relational energy.[46] Before anything else, you must create and show your own energy at work. As the saying goes, enthusiasm is contagious, particularly when it comes from leaders.

It is within your wheelhouse to find out what interests and motivates your people. Sometimes it takes something as small as leaving your door open to begin to communicate this invitation. What inspires your people about the work they do? What is the missing ingredient that, if present, would help propel them through the next threshold of their professional experience? Do they need more challenges? Do they want more support? Are they hungry for training? Do they want to be part of collaborative efforts that will help the company move forward in meaningful ways?

You will be energizing individuals with the trust that you show to team members in a one-on-one relationship, which increases

---

46   Emma Seppälä and Kim Cameron, "The Best Leaders Have a Contagious Positive Energy," *Harvard Business Review*, April 18, 2022, https://hbr.org/2022/04/the-best-leaders-have-a-contagious-positive-energy.

their sense of self-confidence, like in the example of Lakshman from earlier in this chapter. This made him and those involved in his initiative feel liberated and more powerful.

Their energy brought about the initiative that eventually led to the company receiving one of the highest awards for innovation in coatings technology. Such results are about more than just feeling valued, respected, and engaged. When you support and recognize your employees, productivity increases. As a leader, you are a catalyst that helps to produce an abundance of energy going forward.

You must look for ways to authentically engage with employees so they can be inspired, committed, and enthusiastic about their work and the workplace. Remember to ask impactful questions and encourage others to do the same.[47] The questions you ask can give team members a chance to reflect on what they find important. Think of a question as a quest. Where do you want to take your interlocutor with your question? Be willing to broaden your inquiry and explore questions such as the following:

- "What is the most creative idea you heard today?"
- "How do you feel about working with others and taking risks?"

Provide employees with strategic assignments that leverage their expertise and give them opportunities to experience personal and professional growth. Such activities can also be sources of energy. You can cultivate an entrepreneurial spirit by unleash-

---

47   Tijs Besieux, "The Art of Asking Great Questions," *Harvard Business Review*, May 17, 2022, https://hbr.org/2022/05/the-art-of-asking-great-questions.

ing their creativity to establish new ways of working across the organization—a notion that readily takes root in environments where employees feel safe to experiment and explore.

You will energize teams when you help team members build emotional connections among themselves. Give people ways to engage and discover the life-giving forces that others share and value. As a younger employee, Mr. Li from earlier in this chapter embraced the chance to solve a complex challenge. This was a moment when he felt alive.

Years later, Mr. Li relayed his story as a senior engineer and helped all of us discover what he cares about—the very fire that gets his engines going every morning. We would not have learned this had we not heard his story.

Consider the power of stories. Learning about other people builds emotional connections. Connected teams flourish on account of the interactions that members share. Once we understand more about people's interests, hopes, and concerns, we are better equipped to meet their needs. Such information forms the basis for more conversations and the ongoing exchange of stories.

Social scientists have argued that stories "offer windows into personal experience, specifically human agency in life events."[48] Sharing stories unleashes new energy across organizations— energy that cycles back to the storyteller and helps them engage with work in new, exciting ways. Stories have the power to be

48 Catherine K. Reissman, "A Short Story about Long Stories," *Journal of Narrative and Life History* 71, nos. 1–4 (1997): 155–159, https://doi.org/10.1075/jnlh.7.1-4.18ash.

transformative in the sense that they may represent new voices that help us understand life in an organization.[49]

As a leader, you must look at your organization as a system with its own social rituals, such as celebrations, performance reviews, systems, recognition programs, and more.[50] By now, I am willing to bet that you know what an energized organization looks like and how it feels—filled with energy, vibrancy, engagement, and mutual caring.

How is energy created inside of an organization? How does it continue? What drains the energy from an environment? Where do things feel stuck? Where has inertia set in? Think back to a moment in your career when you noticed people coming alive. What motivated them? What caused them to embrace their work and endeavors in new ways? The answers will point back to the things that energize people within an organization, like a two-way charging station that feeds and gains more energy from the grid.

In my career, I have found the Appreciative Inquiry method to be a strong tool to support efforts in this quest. Through this type of inquiry, you safely extract organizational energizers, aspirations, and opportunities, as well as de-energizers. The operating practices of appreciative culture are a critical component of Life Giving Workforce Design.

These practices help build a culture of teamwork, commit-

49   Patrick Ewick and Susan S. Silbey, "Subversive Stories and Hegemonic Tales: Toward a Sociology of Narrative," *Law Society Review* 29, no. 2 (1995): 197–226, https://doi.org/10.2307/3054010.

50   Barry J. Halm, "Life Giving Workforce Design: An Organization Construction That Generates Energy and Capacity for Organizational Effectiveness" (PhD diss., Benedictine University, 2009).

ment to the customer, and a focus on results that permeate the organization. A flourishing environment will always enrich organizational performance,[51] while de-energizing relationships in organizations decrease performance.[52]

At the same time, you will remove things that de-energize your people and the organization. For instance, your insights may lead to changing how the organization handles performance appraisals, streamlines decision-making, organizes projects, or conducts team-building exercises. Understanding strengths, opportunities, and aspirations helps unlock dormant passions that matter most to your people. From there, you can eventually uncover the organization's life-giving forces, as told through the eyes of individuals.

When managers and employees have chances to take on challenging goals and achieve success in the process, you ensure the sustenance of your organization's productive energy and peak performance. Still, sustaining positive energy at the organizational level is a significant challenge that you must continue to nurture with a high level of emotional involvement. You cannot do this alone. Other leaders in your organization must participate with the same dedication and leadership practices to help boost collective energy.

51 Marcial Losada and Emily Heaphy, "The Role of Positivity and Connectivity in the Performance of Business Teams: A Nonlinear Dynamics Model," *American Behavioral Scientist* 47, no. 6 (February 2004): 740–765, https://doi:10.1177/0002764203260208.

52 Alexandra Gerbasi et al., "Destructive De-energizing Relationships: How Thriving Buffers Their Effect on Performance," *Journal of Applied Psychology* 100, no. 5 (2015): 1423–1433, http://dx.doi.org/10.1037/apl0000001.

LET US GET STARTED

You are the master energizer who helps build organizational energy to propel it toward a strategic vision with a high level of performance. Your personal energy, when invested in this process, will light flames under individual employees and create organizational momentum.[53] Toward strengthening your competence in the practice of energizing your organization, I would like to share the following practices:

1. **Discover energy triggers.** Understand your employees' motivations. Discover what triggers their engines. What moments do they live for? How do they feel at moments such as these? Find out what gives them energy and what can prop one door open, then another, then another. When you can discover this energy, you can stoke and nurture it over the long run. To do so, engage them in sharing their stories and learning the stories of others.

2. **Recognize that your organization is a living system.** Discover the context of where life abounds in your organization. What is it about certain orgs, groups, projects, or cultural rituals that inspires life-giving forces to flourish? This type of inquiry will help you discover what generates energy inside the organization. Reflect on management practices and techniques that engage employees to be inspired, committed, and enthusiastic about their work and the workplace. At the same time, discover the things that deplete energy. Use every opportunity to express your joy as a leader. Share your excitement with your team. This can be contagious and will inject positive energy and enthusiasm across teams, and eventually the entire organization.

---

53 Rob Cross, Wayne Baker, and Andrew Parker, "What Creates Energy in Organizations?" *MIT Sloan Management Review* 44, no. 4 (Summer 2003): 51–56.

Chapter 8

CREATE OPPORTUNITIES FOR OTHERS

Legacy is the focus of Chapter 8, and I would like to explore it from a number of angles. To start, when you crack into the word *legacy*, it's natural to think about other people. A legacy does not exist on its own or float around in space. It flows into and through those around us. As leaders, we see it in the actions that employees take and the decisions they make throughout their own careers. Here's something to keep in mind: as a leader, you are one of the most important forces in the journeys your employees take.

As leaders, most of us are motivated by the desire to leave an organization in better shape than we found it. To do so, we must continue to take actions to improve it. Some of our greatest achievements involve the success of those we serve and the knowledge that we have made a difference. When we create opportunities for others, we help them hone their skills, which adds value to the company.

As I have written throughout this book, some employees will seek you out and ask you to give them a chance to be more involved. In many cases, however, we must create opportunities for employees to step up and discover what they are capable of. Whether an opportunity happens as part of a strategic plan or in a pinch, employees want to feel valued and to be challenged. With this in mind, I'd like to share a quick story about a gentleman named Ning Zhu.

WHEN OPPORTUNITY PRESENTS ITSELF AS A NEED

Ning Zhu was an engineer who played a major role in supporting the technology transfer from Japan to the US during my time in North Carolina. If you recall the story from Chapter 2, my mission was to lead the successful transfer and integration of a critical technology from Japan to the US. While doing so, my Japanese counterpart realized the best path forward was to send a member of the US team to Japan in order to learn the technology firsthand.

Ning Zhu was an extremely conscientious professional, but it was clear to me that he was a little bored in his current role, working on the resins side of our business. I had gotten to know him over the course of a few months, and my gut told me this would be a good opportunity for him.

When I presented the idea to him, his response was lukewarm at first. He was worried about having to spend six months in Japan, a country he had never visited, where he had no connections.

He had a young family and did not think that being gone for six months would sit well with his wife. This was 2002, well before smartphones with video call capabilities. Other than pictures, he would not see his family for half of a year, except for perhaps one or two short visits.

It was a Friday when he and I met to discuss the opportunity. I encouraged him to talk it over with his wife and then come to my office early Monday with an update. When Monday came, I could tell that his attitude had shifted when he walked in.

"This is completely new to me," he said, "but I see it as a tremendous growth opportunity. It will be a challenge, but I think I can make it work. I'll do it."

We discussed and established clear and achievable expectations. I assured him of both my guidance and that of my Japanese counterpart.

As I shared in Chapter 2, the technology transfer was a success. Ning played a tremendous role to bring it to fruition and was a positive force in many projects that followed. The thing was, Ning was always a very quiet person. Very few people in the organization saw him as a rising star or someone who would eventually move into a leadership position. In fact, Ning was happy to stay on the resins side of the business. In his mind, taking a quiet and consistent route was the best approach to guaranteeing job security, which mattered very much to him, considering his young family.

During the transfer, Ning literally became a bridge between Japanese and US operations. In the process, he extended himself well beyond his comfort zone as a person and as a professional. The work was completely outside the range of what he'd been doing. However, knowing how critical the technology transfer was, he put all of his energy into learning the digital printing resin technology and trusting his Japanese counterparts.

I visited Japan twice during Ning's stay. On both visits, as well as during his one visit back to the US, I could see how much more confident and motivated he was about the project and about his involvement. Afterward, when the transfer was complete, Ning harnessed this excitement and gave a series of lectures to other members of the company, where he discussed everything he learned in Japan—both personally and professionally.

Upon his return, I invited him to reflect on his experience and discuss how the process made him feel, what his challenges were, and how he overcame them. He explained how the opportunity motivated him to extend himself in completely new ways. He admitted that he had at first been apprehensive but that his Japanese counterparts adopted him as a trusted coworker. As for the results, he was happy to see that the company reaped the financial benefits of the technology in the US digital printing resins markets, growing that side of business from 16 percent to 24 percent within a few years.

Months after the transfer was complete, Ning and I were having a friendly conversation, when he asked, "Now that the technology transfer is over, I'd like to ask, why did you pick me?"

"Because I knew you could do it," I said. "And also, I wanted you to see that you don't need others to see you as a rising star in order to rise. This opportunity was there for you, and you took it on."

EMBRACE EXPERIMENTATION

When creating opportunities for others, you must be open to experimentation. An organization is like a big laboratory. You have to continually experiment to discover what you can create. In a space of creative experimentation, you can't be overly critical of team members or hem people in based on the constraints of job descriptions. Instead, identify areas where people either already possess an ability or where they would enjoy a chance to contribute and grow. How else will you know which employees can rise to the occasion unless you test them?

Experimentation is not easy, and being open to creating opportunities does not come naturally for some leaders. Many would rather find their way into and through a system that works and stay with the dynamics that currently exist. This reminds me of something I experienced early in my career, when my department head used to assign us additional responsibilities in areas outside our formal job responsibilities. In the beginning it was nerve-racking and disruptive, and I didn't see the point. Looking back, I see how the disruption was actually quite valuable. It allowed each of us a chance to broaden, grow, adapt, and figure out what we were good at, and eventually even great at.

Some employees ask to be put in a position of influence and lead a strategic project, similar to Jim from Chapter 1. When I met Jim, the word was already out about him in the organization: "He's not creative enough to succeed here." Much to his credit, Jim felt differently about his status as a creative professional. He wanted to move up from the role of engineer and grow into the position of a project manager. In his mind, he had the organizational skills, along with an understanding of the ins and outs involved. He asked for the opportunity to apply his talents toward specific outcomes. What I needed to do was to help him refine his talents in a way that would help others see his capabilities and potential.

Other employees need to be engaged or coaxed into taking on something new—similar to Ning in the anecdote above. Or like a gentleman named Joerg Unger, who was another direct report of mine during my time in Ohio. Joerg was involved in sales for a technology he was helping to develop. I saw something about Joerg that others did not see and found ways to create opportunities for him so that others could recognize his potential. Taking these types of actions as a leader helps employees realize new potential and also helps the organization take advantage of new skills and acumen. In the end, your people and your firm both flourish.

COACHING PEOPLE UP

Coaching is a process of helping people be their best, equipping them with knowledge and opportunities they need to progress and succeed. Being able to be a coach for someone begins by building the types of interpersonal relationships I have been writing about since the start of this book. That is because coaching is a process that is based on interpersonal relationships.

When you show an interest in someone, you build their confidence and competence. I'm not talking about giving lip service or looking for a polite way to pass the time while waiting for coffee to brew. These types of conversations must happen at the level of true engagement, where you focus on a person's individual needs and engage them in the process of learning.

When you begin to coach someone, you must enter the experience with the belief that they will make the right choices if given an opportunity. As they engage with you, they will trust you as someone who can help them build new competencies and confidence. This, in turn, will help to generate their own reflective capacity as they begin to expand their skills.

As a coach, your job is not to solve problems, but to help others think through their challenges. This reminds me of a young man named Prashant Gupta, a senior manager during my time in India. Prashant wanted to move up in the organization and approached me to help him do so. To get started, we explored a number of areas and opportunities and discussed growth possibilities. He was fixated on making monetary gains in his career, which he saw as the ultimate outcome. I encouraged him to take a step back and look at the process involved in arriving at such an outcome.

As we worked more and more, I helped him broaden his professional network by connecting him with people he could learn from. I also encouraged him to learn outside of his current role and to get involved in other initiatives in order to stretch and strengthen his capabilities. In addition, I recommended him for a high-profile assignment, which helped him develop stronger relationships with senior managers.

One of the most important pieces of our work involved the topic of his legacy, something he had not thought about prior to coaching. "What are the lasting contributions you would like to make to this organization?" I asked him. "And how can you align these contributions with your future decisions?"

My point in asking him about his legacy was to help him shift his focus toward himself as a person. Beyond career advancement, I wanted him to see coaching as an exercise in personal development and growth. "To be a leader," I explained, "you must understand who you are, as well as who you must be."

DEVELOPING GREAT PEOPLE

Leaders can emerge at any level of the organization, but without engaged and committed people, you will not produce new leaders. However, if you can successfully bring your vision to the fore and find ways to motivate and perpetuate the achievements of others, leaders will step forward.

There are many formal leadership training programs, of course, but I believe that future leaders must have a stake in organizational leadership, or at least the opportunity to co-create opportunities along the way.[54] As a current leader, you must be able to focus on behaviors that could help foster a positive climate filled with psychological safety if you want future leaders to begin to take root. When you invest your efforts and energy in others—when you show them that you care—you will create an environment of sustained engagement and commitment.

Engagement never goes away. It is a constant and, in my view, a necessity. By engaging others and inspiring them to develop their capabilities to lead, you establish what leadership means in your organization. Getting to know people within your org sets the foundation for this type of work. It creates inroads as you seek to identify those who have potential to lead. From there, it

54 David V. Day, "Leadership Development: A Review in Context," *Leadership Quarterly* 11, no. 4 (2001): 581–613, https://psycnet.apa.org/doi/10.1016/S1048-9843(00)00061-8.

is your job as a leader to help them rise up to the point where they go from proving themselves to moving to the next level.

REFLECTIONS

When growth opportunities are abundant and the doors are open, employees find more energy and inspiration. Naturally, there may be some level of apprehension at the idea of something new. Still, as you help people walk through their nerves, you bolster their strength to enter uncharted territories and discover their own greater potential.[55]

Employees who attach importance to personal growth and development will stretch themselves and strive to do better in their jobs.[56] If they have a high motivation for development opportunities and recognize the psychological safety you have created through engagement and trust, they will find ways to invest in themselves and say yes to opportunities that push boundaries.

As you engage with employees, you begin to understand the types of challenges that can help middle performers step up into new roles. Through this lens, you can look for ways to connect average performers with higher performers and involve them in small-group initiatives. Taking these types of steps can lead to a twofold impact: as you create opportunities for average performers to learn from high performers, you also give high

55   James E. Maddux, "Self-Efficacy: The Power of Believing You Can," in *The Oxford Handbook of Positive Psychology*, ed. Shane J. Lopez and C. R. Snyder (New York: Oxford University Press, 2011), 335–344, https://doi.org/10.1093/oxfordhb/9780195187243.013.0031.

56   Yanfei Wang, Yi Chen, and Yu Zhu, "Promoting Innovative Behavior in Employees: The Mechanism of Leader Psychological Capital," *Frontiers in Psychology* 11 (January 2021): 598090, https://www.frontiersin.org/articles/10.3389/fpsyg.2020.598090/full.

performers a chance to mentor other workers, thus setting them up for future coaching roles.

As a leader, you must exhibit a mindset of abundance, see employees as unlimited resources, and show them that success is available to anyone. This way of thinking opens doors to unlimited possibilities. When you give people the space to create and the chance to lead, they will prove themselves capable of taking fantastic leaps forward.[57] They will shift the way they see challenges and understand that hard work is the path toward self-fulfillment and growth.

Following this path will not be the end of their journey, but rather the beginning of something new and vastly different. When people show that they are ready to take the reins, they tend to stay hungry; they remember the last experience for a long time, develop an increased sense of self-awareness, and look for ways to feed their desire for more new opportunities. This type of excitement cycles back to benefit the organization like an influx of supercharged energy.[58]

Something else happens as well. Other employees begin to look for their own growth opportunities, which brings even more energy to the organization. Suddenly, opportunities become abundant, and people continue to look for ways to feed the energy around them. Naturally, when they know that you are invested in their success, this adds yet another boost to the new

---

57   Kate Dames, "The Missing Key to a Productive and Engaged Team," *People Development Magazine,* April 22, 2022, https://peopledevelopmentmagazine.com/2022/04/22/the-missing-key-productive-engaged-team/.

58   Urim Retkoceri, "Remembering Emotions," *Biology & Philosophy* 37, no. 5 (February 2022): 1–26, https://doi.org/10.1007/s10539-022-09834-5.

levels of engagement and commitment that are happening all around you.

You will never know who your next great contributor is until you get to know your people. Without the engagement and energy pieces, how will you know what opportunities align with what people? There is only so much information you can gain from a résumé. You must be willing to engage and to stay engaged over and over.

LET US GET STARTED

Creating opportunities for others increases their confidence and self-determination and helps them develop greater competence. People will perform their best when you provide them with chances to exceed their own expectations.[59] As you strengthen your competency in the practice of creating opportunities for others, I'd like to recommend the following practices:

1. **Gain insights on employees.** Engage your employees so that you can understand their needs. Ask questions outside their regular project updates on skills they would like to update, areas they find most challenging, and projects they would like to be part of. Practice active listening and be curious. Development conversations represent an opportunity to get insights into what keeps them going or next steps to keep them engaged and growing.

2. **Create more experiential learning.** Look for opportunities to help employees develop new skills. While learning, engage employees so that they internalize those learning

59 James M. Kouzes and Barry Z. Posner, *Everyday People, Extraordinary Leadership: How to Make a Difference Regardless of Your Title, Role, or Authority* (Hoboken: John Wiley & Sons, 2021).

moments, which can be small or big, and build confidence. Provide regular feedback on what they are doing well and where there may be opportunities for improvement.

Chapter 9

COMPLETE A BOLD, INNOVATIVE INITIATIVE

A vision of the future is just that—a vision. Having a vision is merely the start. Achieving the vision is a completely different scenario. However, when your vision has a strong foundation to begin with, you are more prepared to move toward the future state. You cannot define boldness by the vision alone. You need to execute that vision with a series of bold initiatives that are more concrete and are framed for the audience you need to convince.

Taking on a bold initiative involves rallying people around a common goal. It is the focal point to define strategies for achieving a better future. As you are shaping up a bold initiative, you need to solicit the involvement of employees. Here in Chapter 9, I'd like to return to India and share the journey we took toward creating a vision of being a sustainable operation that dramatically cut down on harmful materials and began moving in a new, greener direction.

INSIGHT AND EXPERIMENTATION

In Chapter 5, I mentioned that I had the opportunity to attend one of the first green chemistry workshops in our industry, where Dr. John Warner, president of the Warner Babcock Institute for Green Chemistry, was a keynote speaker. I was intrigued by his presentation and his knowledge, and when I returned to the office, I was convinced that our company could indeed pivot toward a green future. However, we needed much more insight if we were actually going to be able to pull it off.

One of my managers who had been helping from the start was very excited. "Why don't you contact Dr. Warner in Boston?" I said. "Find out what we need to do to learn more about this approach."

As it turned out, Dr. Warner was warm and extremely amenable. He was an expert in his field but did not know much about our actual products—in a way, he was excited to learn from us as well. In short order, he had invited our team to visit him in Boston for a week. Our goal was to learn as much as we could in order to apply it to what we were trying to accomplish back in India.

Four members from our cohort flew to Boston to spend a week with Dr. Warner. They were from different areas of the company's portfolio, which was an important detail. They were also eager to move in this direction and had put in their fair share of time exploring green opportunities. If the company was going to transform across the entirety of its portfolio, we would need insight and enthusiasm coming from every possible direction.

When the team returned from Boston, they felt extremely energized and empowered to begin testing various principles. They were ready to see how close we were and how much work we needed to do in order to actually make the business case. Some early experiments in the laboratories did not pan out. Others did but would not scale in a way that would produce large enough cost savings. However, these experiences were not failures. They helped us establish a very necessary baseline in terms of understanding the toxicity of our products and raw materials—one I would eventually return to when it was time to make the business case.

As they continued to learn and apply green trends toward actually improving our products, and eventually creating a green portfolio, I put the bulk of my attention into building and presenting the business case.

TRANSLATING THE VISION

When I first listened to Dr. Warner, I knew that if we could apply even a portion of what he discussed, we would be well on our way to transforming our entire portfolio, and perhaps our organization in the process. This thought led to other thoughts, which helped the idea begin to form into a shape. Still, I could not simply pitch the company on transforming toward a green portfolio on the grounds that it was the right thing to do. Dr. Warner's insights helped me see the business applications, which pointed back to reducing waste, chemical by-products, and the costs we were sinking toward the constant churn of mitigation.

From our own independent research, along with what we had learned from Dr. Warner, the facts of the business case were evident. In the long run, green chemistry was a more cost-effective way to do business. Yes, there may be front-end costs associated with transformation, but the results would lead to less toxicity, fewer by-products, and an overall process that would save us money. And, of course, our future products would be safer for the environment.

I requested a meeting with the chairman and senior leadership. I told them I wished to present a proposal to explore a green portfolio for our line of decorative products at the highest level and asked for a spot on the executive committee's next meeting agenda. Then, little more than a week later, along with one of my managers and a senior scientist, I took the next step in presenting the vision and met with the members of the committee.

"What I am proposing here is to develop a green portfolio of products," I began. I didn't get past the first slide before a hand shot up in the room.

"There's no need for this," one gentleman said. "There are no regulations in this part of the world." Then another hand went into the air. "This would be impossible for us to do. Imagine the expenses. It will put us out of business!"

Calmly I replied, "If you'll allow me to explain the rationale behind the proposal, I hope to make a convincing case that addresses both of these concerns." I continued and presented everything my team and I had gathered to date: the issues related to our current portfolio; the waste we were creating to date; the costs we were sinking into our current mitigation efforts; the global trends toward green solutions; and the fact that, despite our pledge to be an innovative company, the market did not see us as innovative.

"My friends, it's only a matter of time before these market forces conspire to be our undoing," I said. "If your concerns are related to the cost of action, let me ask this: What is the cost of inaction?"

I could see that some members of the board were mulling this over, while others remained unconvinced. To his credit, the chairman understood. However, he was not ready to move forward without full executive committee approval to do so.

"Let's try something," I suggested. "Why don't we discuss the reasons why you feel we cannot do this, point for point. Let's spend a few minutes looking at why you believe we cannot eliminate carcinogenic materials without increasing costs, for instance. I believe that if we can spend time on each concern, we can find a solution together."

The board agreed to play along, and for close to an hour we approached every angle—costs, global implications, manpower, resources.

"Mosongo," the chairman said at one point, "this is indeed a noble challenge. Can you walk us through again the work you and your team have done to date?"

"Happily," I agreed. I spoke in greater detail about Dr. Warner's influence, in addition to the testing we had already begun. I continued and described the framework we planned to use in the selection of raw materials and the design of new products. I also created space for my manager and senior scientist to offer their insights and to field questions. The executive committee was especially interested in what our team had uncovered about carcinogens and what paths we could follow to eliminate them.

"How do you envision beginning?" one of the board members asked. "Where are the early wins and the low-hanging fruit?"

"What if we start only with one brand and go from there?" another board member suggested. Suddenly, the tenor of the room began to shift. Now, not only were they asking questions; they were also offering suggestions and making recommendations.

By the time we left the meeting, we had earned the committee's approval to continue. It was a moment to celebrate, but certainly not the end of our journey. Senior managers were excited, especially since the vision and bold initiative had come from our group rather than being directed from the top-down. Now we needed to bring the entire company together to introduce them to the vision and galvanize our efforts in that direction. And to do so required something more than words, promises, or even data. We needed something memorable—a vision that people could see, feel, and imagine their way into.

ROLLING OUT THE BOLD INITIATIVE

My team and I brainstormed as we built and reviewed a more in-depth presentation deck. We thought again and again about a way to get people excited to be involved in executing the initiative. We kept coming back to the notion that the initiative, while set in the present moment, was really about the future, feeding off of the grand vision of sustainability. What could we tell people or, better yet, show them, about this future? After all, we weren't fortune tellers. But we did have the gift of creativity on our side. And knowing this, a light bulb went on.

"You know," I said, "we actually could show them the future by showing them the news from the future."

A week later, the day of the town hall meeting was incredibly warm. It was a rare occasion for every employee to gather at once, but despite the heat, people found their way into the conference room in their groups. Sitting at the front of the room with my team, it was easy to feel the anticipation, not to mention a bit of anxiety.

"Well," I said to them, "this is the moment." After a brief introduction, I launched into our presentation's first slide. Instead of environmental regulations, promises, or graphs, the image that greeted the room was a clipping of the front page of the *Times of India*, one of the largest newspapers in the country by circulation. With the help of some simple graphic design skills, I'd altered the date, along with some of the column copy. The fictionalized headline, set five years in the future, was announcing major changes in our organization as if they had already happened: according to the copy, we had successfully created and launched our market's most technologically advanced green coatings system and were now on the forefront of revolutionizing our entire industry.

For a moment, there was a puzzled silence in the room, then a bit of murmuring. Then, with everyone living in the future state, I backtracked to the present and challenged them to work toward transforming our portfolio into a green one within five years.

"We have a chance to do something very special as a company," I began, "something that no other competitor throughout Asia and very few throughout the world are doing."

STEPPING TOWARD THE FUTURE

When you set a bold, compelling goal for an organization, people get excited. That was the case as we moved forward with our green portfolio initiative. Team members began to rally around it and volunteer themselves to help. One scientist began calling weekly meetings during which we could assess our progress.

A new level of collaborative energy emerged across the organization as we mapped out weekly and monthly goals, what the next quarter would look like, which pilot to run first, and so on. This collaborative energy was the result of deep employee engagement and appreciative senior leaders who nurtured and supported collaborations with a clear focus.

During this time, I was struck by the transformation the company had undergone in little more than eighteen months. It started as a desire to open doors. From there, a small group of eager employees and I found ways to reconfigure the way people worked across teams. Then, with this new energy in place, the vision of a green portfolio began to galvanize. Now the entire company was moving in unison toward this bold vision.

Fulfilling a vision takes time, but when others around you support your vision—and when the business case is clear—very powerful things begin to happen. When I first went to the board, I presented a vision that, if executed, would lead to major changes to the brand. We could not simply wave a wand and make our existing portfolio green. We needed to construct an entirely new portfolio. In the process, we had the potential to become an industry leader in developing green products—not just in the Asian market, but globally.

Our work on the portfolio also shifted the way others inside of the company viewed our organization. As we took efforts to disallow and eventually do away with certain compounds in our formulations, the rest of the company followed suit. Soon our group began educating others in the company, including a series of lectures and thought shares on the benefits of shifting toward green strategies.

Slowly, and sometimes reluctantly, groups and departments involved in supply chain, marketing, and purchasing began pursuing ways to become greener in their own efforts—switching to energy-efficient fuel types, cutting down on paper usage, increasing recycling efforts, and choosing more eco-conscious vendors when they could. Ripples such as these began to extend beyond the vision I had first presented to executives and were evidence of a gravitational pull and collective yearning that I hadn't even considered.

Today, the company continues to lead this space with green, environmentally friendly paintings and coatings. But again, there was no wand waving. The path we followed continued along the same course as the foundation: small steps, one after another. In this way, we were able to maintain momentum and piece together the journey that did indeed lead to the envisioned future. In the process, many in the organization turned into corporate evangelists for sustainability.

REFLECTIONS

When people believe in something—and when they share a vision—the mind will find the way. To launch and complete a bold initiative, leaders must be purposeful. They must also take action. In doing so, they must also remember an old adage: alone you may go faster, but together you will go farther.

Communicating a vision and the why behind it is a major piece of the equation. However, you must also include clear goals and actions to help people understand what it will take to carry the initiative out. Otherwise, they will become disengaged. By regularly sharing information, people will continue to connect with the same passion and drive they felt at the start and will continue to work accordingly.

The leadership journey does not happen in isolation. The vision I have shared throughout this chapter was tied to a number of other stages that happened earlier and involved people at every step: opening doors, listening, reorganizing, galvanizing, energizing, motivating, directing.[60] The mix of appreciative management practices, engaged employees, and the focus on delivering quality products generated energy and enthusiasm that fed the work and spiraled throughout the organization. Again and again, the collective energy and willingness of the

---

60   Nitin Nohria, Boris Groysberg, and Linda-Eling Lee, "Employee Motivation; A Powerful New Model," *Harvard Business Review,* July–August 2008, https://hbr.org/2008/07/employee-motivation-a-powerful-new-model.

group continued to grow. The strength of this energy revealed what can happen when energized employees work to achieve a common goal.

In the story I've shared, my team members were enthusiastic and could see the opportunity for a green portfolio. However, initially the company had difficulty fully embracing the initiative. This was understandable, as this change required some senior leaders to make mental leaps and open their minds to the idea of changing the company's core identity. As these leaders began to see the distant opportunity, the rest of the organization did the same. Still, resistance in various pockets was stubborn at times, especially since the company's market position was so entrenched.

In this type of situation, leaders of significance must put on their "practicing psychologist" hats. You have to be able to manage your own thought process as well as those of others.

Before my team and I could get the company to fully embrace the green portfolio vision, we had to gain the respect of colleagues in other parts of the organization, especially those who had long operated in the existing dynamic. In the process, it was important to demonstrate two things. First, we needed to develop one product that met all the performance and cost constraints. Second, we needed to develop it fast, using our existing processing technology.

For the company, the move toward a green portfolio was a tremendous success. One key to our success involved the comprehensive approach we took to the entire development cycle, from raw materials to the final products. I have already shared a number of critical business outcomes going back to this book's introduction. In short, every choice and decision we made put us ahead of our competition, which is where the company remains today.

One moment of great satisfaction for me and for the entire organization, which still lingers with me even as I write, was the development and commercialization of a completely green architectural paint for interior applications. The paint contained no volatile organic compounds and consisted of better attributes than all incumbent products. I was amazed to watch that particular vision come to life. It was a major undertaking, and the team received international kudos for the development of this product.

How did we get there? Persistence and perseverance were certainly part of the equation. And let's not forget willpower, which involves a personal commitment to making something happen. These are the ingredients that give people and teams the energy to overcome barriers. You must engage with people at the level where their personal motivation resides if you wish to unleash their true spirits.[61]

At the same time, openness, experimentation, and a willingness to seek guidance were also key. The bold initiative communicated great potential for innovation, and as a result generated a lot of organizational energy. The challenge provided employees an opportunity to dream. Easy problems never excite, but challenging ones do.

---

61   Sumantra Bruch and Sumantra Ghoshal, "The Bold Decisive Manager: Cultivating a Company of Action-Takers," *Ivey Business Journal*, July–August 2004, https://iveybusinessjournal.com/publication/the-bold-decisive-manager-cultivating-a-company-of-action-takers/.

When you consider the idea of completing a bold initiative, ask yourself: Who are your champions? Where are your blind spots? What information do you need to build a strong base before you take the message up the chain? In the case of launching our green portfolio, I knew I could rely on three or four enthusiastic managers who remained determined and also undeterred when challenges arrived. There was no quit in them, and their enthusiasm helped me to maintain my own focus and grit. They were the core team of those fast zebras. I take my hat off to them.

When it is time to march forward with your own bold initiative, be sure that your team members have your back and that they understand the many details and nuances involved. This will come in handy when it is time to take the message up the chain of command and out to more people within the organization. You also need to ensure that teams operate as more than the sum of their parts. For that, you need to recognize that teams are inherently social and require members with emotional intelligence to achieve a high level of productivity.[62]

Remember that there will be times when work becomes tedious and less exciting than imagining, building, and pitching the vision. This is a natural state that happens in the course of any endeavor. In our own experience, we continued to march forward with the vision as the driving force, so when the work felt less exciting, we knew how and where to connect it. For example, we conducted surveys at different times as a way of checking in with employees and consistently found strong alignment with what the organization was doing and what our people wanted. In that way, the vision itself reminded us that while certain steps

62   Ben Weidmann and David J. Deming, "Team Players: How Social Skills Improve Team Performance," *Econometrica* 89, no. 6 (November 2021): 2637–2657, https://doi.org/10.3982/ECTA18461.

may have felt tedious, following through on the larger initiative was well worth the effort.

Bold initiatives have a way of happening when you break them down into phases—reaching for the low-hanging fruit, if you will, or stacking wins atop of wins.[63] However you break things down, it's worth remembering three things:

1. Conduct regular debriefs. These improve team performance.[64]
2. Recognize top performance. This raises standards and further increases the performance of the entire team.[65]
3. Celebrate small wins. This builds a sense of community spirit and renews the organizational energy to move forward.[66]

LET US GET STARTED

When you take on a bold, inspiring initiative, you discover new ways to motivate and invigorate employees, especially those who support the initiative early on. Soon individuals and teams begin to move in a synchronized fashion.[67] At the same time,

---

63 Teresa M. Amabile and Steven J. Kramer, *The Progress Principle: Using Small Wins to Ignite Joy, Engagement, and Creativity at Work* (Boston: Harvard Business Press, 2011).

64 Joseph Andrew Allen et al., "Debriefs: Teams Learning from Doing in Context," *American Psychologist* 73, no. 4 (May–June 2018): 504–516, http://dx.doi.org/10.1037/amp0000246.

65 Christiane Bradler et al., "Employee Recognition and Performance: A Field Experiment," *Management Science* 62, no. 11 (February 2016), https://doi.org/10.1287/mnsc.2015.2291.

66 Tiffany McDowell, Sheba Ehteshami, and Kyle Sandell. "Are You Having Fun Yet?" *Deloitte Review*, January 2019, https://www2.deloitte.com/xe/en/insights/topics/talent/making-work-fun-competitive-advantage.html.

67 Bernhard Schmid and Jonathan Adams, "Motivation in Project Management: The Project Manager's Perspective," *Project Management Journal* 39, no. 2 (June 2008): 60–71, https://doi:10.1002/pmj.20042.

no matter how inspired your project is, the execution is critical. Without it, frustration sets in.

If you want to accomplish your goals and bring your initiative to life, the execution depends on how you lead. As you work toward strengthening your competence in the practice of completing a bold, innovative initiative, I'd like to offer a couple of practices:

1. **Be a marketing manager for the initiative.** Promote the initiative that encapsulates your vision, just like a marketing manager would do with customers, by articulating the compelling vision, project purpose, and benefits. This engages key stakeholders. Be a savvy marketer to ensure that all parties at all levels in your organization and across the company understand and internalize the promise of the project.
2. **Plan and deliver.** Along with your team, craft and share a plan with a broader set of stakeholders, including marketing, manufacturing, and operations. Their inputs will help improve the plan. Be transparent throughout the process. At launch, make a big deal of the merit of the project. You embody the initiative. Regularly communicate progress and performance. This keeps the hope and expectations you have built from being demolished. Debrief, recognize top performers, celebrate small milestones, and invite other stakeholders to join in the celebration.

Chapter 10

ENABLE OTHERS
TO LEAD

Leadership does not happen in a silo. It involves team members at every turn. When you develop leaders throughout other levels of the organization—and when you enable them to lead on their own—you create a foundation on which your own vision becomes reality. As a leader, if you are truly looking to create an impact, leave a legacy, and be remembered, then developing others so that they can lead must be at the center of your journey. In the words of Jim Collins, "Great vision without great people is irrelevant."[68] In Chapter 10, I'd like to share my thoughts on the team aspect of leadership.

LEADERSHIP IS NOT A SOLO VENTURE

During the early stages of my career, our vice president liked to meet with our managerial team at the end of the week, usually

---

68   Jim Collins, *Good to Great: Why Some Companies Make the Leap...and Others Don't* (New York: Harper Collins, 2001), 42.

late on a Friday. He would ask each of us to discuss the various highs and lows, things we had learned, what was coming up next week, etc. None of us actually looked forward to these conversations. In fact, we were often afraid of these moments, especially at the end of the week when we didn't feel like we had much energy to put toward reflection or to talk about successes and failures.

Still, these conversations were a chance to learn from each other and also to hold ourselves accountable. Typically we would talk about projects and approach our answers from a classical management perspective: numbers, deliverables, benchmarks, and the like. During one particular meeting, as we went around the room, I could see the VP was growing agitated. Suddenly, he cut someone off mid-sentence.

"I don't want to hear about your projects," he said. "I want to hear about the things you are doing to help your people succeed. How else are you actually going to learn from each other, if all you do is talk about projects and deliverables? I want to hear about your people. How are you setting them up to lead?"

This was a powerful moment for me. I was still very new in my leadership journey, and even though I felt deeply connected to the people part of leadership, I had not thought of it as something to discuss with our group. But our VP was right, and his question was valid: What were we doing to enable others? How were we helping them become leaders?

Leadership is not about how far we progress. Rather, it is about how far we help others progress. In my experience, high-potential individuals seek and enjoy first-time challenges. They are eager to learn, develop new skills, and incorporate learnings into their portfolio of competencies.

Perhaps, through engagement, empathy, and listening, you have identified such individuals who possess the potential for greater responsibility or picked up on characteristics and behaviors that support trust and engagement. Perhaps you have even built strong working relationships with these employees and are actively helping them in their own leadership development. Those of high potential may be lightly challenged in the organization. In some cases, they may not be in visible roles.

Keep in mind that not all people are equally gifted in their ability to lead. However, I believe that everyone can grow and develop leadership abilities and that their perspectives and experiences affect what they incorporate in the development process.

One of the reasons why some leaders are afraid to develop others is because they perceive that if they enable others to lead, they might lose their own control. After all, if you let someone else take the reins, aren't you training your future replacement? These leaders might also be worried that they won't get the recognition they deserve for someone else's success. Or perhaps they are worried that they simply don't know how to enable someone else. This type of uncertainty might have to do with a lack of confidence or the feeling that you are not quite ready to be the kind of leader who would do these things. You might even be concerned that this or that person is not yet ready to step into a bigger role and that their failure will reflect poorly on you.

When I was first asked to lead, I was more than a little uncertain.

In fact, at certain times I was downright frightened. And while my VP expressed confidence in me, his approach left me in a position where I still had to figure things out for myself. "You'll be fine," was his mantra. In retrospect, allowing me to make choices and use my best judgment was an act of trust.

SCALE UP YOUR IMPACT

Believe it or not, one of the keys to building your leadership legacy is to develop and empower other leaders. In essence, you scale up your impact by multiplying creativity and talents. There are many ways to achieve this, and from my experience, it occurs via a combination of approaches.

First, you must delegate authority and allow for autonomy. When people receive genuine autonomy, they feel powerful, which motivates them to bring about their full capabilities. Remember, your trust and clarity will help them be successful. As a leader, one of the greatest ways to extend trust comes from giving people a chance to take charge, starting with taking charge of themselves.

A related piece of the legacy puzzle involves building and conveying a sense of confidence. Neuroscience tells us that confidence has a multiplying effect and that when people feel the confidence of others, they are more confident in their own ability to go beyond their comfort zone.[69] Along these lines, you must also be clear in your expectations. Trust and confidence without clarity can lead to frustration and confusion, both of

---

69   Dominic S. Fareri, Luke J. Chang, and Mauricio R. Delgado, "Computational Substrates of Social Value in Interpersonal Collaboration," *Journal of Neuroscience* 35, no. 21 (May 2015): 8170–8180, https://doi.org/10.1523%2FJNEUROSCI.4775-14.2015.

which erode trust and create fear. Any relationship based on fear, or where trust is lacking, will not promote a positive legacy.

Second, you must also find ways to provide a platform for challenges. Difficult or trying experiences can stretch people in ways that allow them to grow and strengthen their capabilities. One challenging experience alone will not support individual development. As the saying goes, experience is indeed the best teacher. So give them experiences that challenge them. Then give them space and opportunity to reflect on the challenges and find the lessons.

In the process, you must also provide support and share feedback. As a leader of significance, I encourage you to strive to do both at as high a level as possible. Your future leaders will not know how they are doing if you do not give them feedback and help them understand the consequences of their work. With insight, they can improve. In fact, when your insight differs from how an employee perceives an experience, it can help them gain a more well-rounded sense of their qualities and how they need to grow.[70]

In my early days as a manager, I could provide challenging opportunities, but I used to fall short on offering strong feedback. If you recall from Chapter 1, my approachability is what gave Jim the confidence he needed to knock on my door and ask for an opportunity. Jim's story is one of success. Enabled to lead with a challenging project, he eventually worked his way into becoming a very strong and successful manager.

---

70 Francesca Gino, "Research: We Drop People Who Give Us Critical Feedback," *Harvard Business Review*, September 16, 2016, https://hbr.org/2016/09/research-we-drop-people-who-give-us-critical-feedback.

For me, I had to work hard in the early days of my management career to strengthen the way I offered feedback and criticism. I could not find the right balance between the part of me that sought to engage and the part of me that needed to be more assertive, so to say. I had to develop it as I went.

Whenever I brought this up to my vice president, he would smile and say things like "Mosongo, you know what you need to do; you just need to do it." I quickly realized that providing the wrong kind of feedback does not help an employee or the organization. And, as you might suspect, no one really wants to give negative feedback, but people are actually ready to hear it.[71]

Third, and most important for your leadership legacy, when bringing future leaders along, you must help them learn to learn from their experiences. This is a tricky one. How does a person actually develop the skill where they are learning to learn?

Actually, a person can learn to learn by being reflective. This idea may be uncomfortable for people who are attached to their subject matter expertise and don't want to extend themselves. After all, going beyond our experience thresholds can be uncomfortable for anyone. But when people do, they must also be able to reflect on how it felt to go beyond their comfort and to be in a situation where they did not know the answers. This requires a growth mindset, regardless of where they are in a company's org chart.

Building a reflective capacity involves self-knowledge, self-awareness, and opportunities to explore intentionality. Encourage

---

71   Gino, "Research."

future leaders to reflect on how each day goes, what was missing, and how they want tomorrow to turn out. It is important that you take them on this journey of reflection so that they can learn from their own experiences and become wiser along the way. Once they start asking reflective questions of themselves, they can move forward and begin to address things that are more complex and difficult.

TAKING INCREASED RESPONSIBILITY

When promoting an employee, the new role will present brand-new challenges and most likely cause them to adopt a much different approach than they had been using in their previous position. One particular employee named Miguel comes to mind when I think about a person's struggle with becoming a senior manager.

Miguel was a high-potential manager with five years of experience leading a marketing group and technical service for one of our divisions. He had helped to expand the market share of the previous segment and was promoted as director to include product development and sales for emerging technologies. In his new position, he was suddenly in charge of twenty people. I wanted him to be able to extend his management experience to product development with the help of an experienced team of managers below him. However, after a few months, it became apparent that Miguel was struggling with taking on this role.

I had to find out how I could help him make the transition from specialist to generalist, and from tactical to strategic. He wanted to restructure his department and received quite a bit of resistance in his efforts. In the ensuing weeks, I saw him lose confidence and naturally gravitate toward things he had done before rather than continue to try something new. He did not realize that the things that had gotten him here would not help him go forward.

One day he came into my office, clearly frustrated, shut the door behind him, and sat down in a heap. He didn't say anything, so I spoke first.

"They don't know what you are trying to do," I said. "The change is driving them crazy. You need to appreciate that different groups approach these types of issues in different ways. Your old approaches are not going to work with them." To his credit, Miguel was receptive to this feedback and appreciated the new perspective.

With my feedback in his mind, Miguel began asking other people for theirs as well, including direct reports and peers. He took the sum of our insights and began to shift his focus toward areas of strength as well as spaces for improvement. In turn, his team members began to seek his feedback and opinions on how they could work better together.

It is not easy to reach a level of mutual respect and trust. However, this story ended well. For Miguel, his willingness to have open discussions with team members paid off handsomely for all of us. To get there, it required a strong level of engagement. More than anything, Miguel's ability to hear my feedback kicked off the change. After he found his footing, he stopped by my office and shared a quote from Albert Einstein: "No problem can be solved from the same level of consciousness that created it."

EXTENDING THE BOUNDARIES OF THE JOB

The chance to practice leadership in real situations can extend beyond the realm of senior managers. Employees at lower levels deserve opportunities as well. This reminds me of two young engineers I once managed, Carlos and Steve. Our company was in a sticky situation with one of our largest customers. They were having difficulties using formulations we had created for them. They were in the automotive industry, and their mounting complaints of our formulations did not bode well for our future.

No one could figure out the cause of the problem, but the issue needed to be solved urgently. If we ignored it much longer, we would lose the client. Carlos and Steve were aware of the dynamics and the stakes, and the pressure was very high.

I assigned Steve to lead the charge to find a solution and brought in Carlos, who was highly skilled in processing these particular plastics, to assist. They were both hungry to prove themselves, but neither had received a chance just yet.

Together, they decided to visit the customer directly. They flew to Houston to meet with their technicians on the shop floor. After their first meeting, Carlos and Steve brought back the data, and we attempted to recreate the customer's issue inside of our facilities. However, no matter what we tried, we could not replicate the situation.

Back in Houston for a second visit, Carlos and Steve dug deeper and discovered something the customer had not shared: they were putting undue stress on the material we'd fabricated for them and using it in ways for which it was not designed. Carlos and Steve only discovered this issue because they had taken it upon themselves to visit the customer's facility on multiple occasions and work directly with their technicians.

Uncovering the truth behind the customer's issue did much more than salvage our relationship with them. It actually led us to create a new formulation on their behalf and launch a new type of working arrangement with them. This was no routine task.

For Carlos and Steve, the experience translated into making a meaningful connection with the customer when it counted. The customer placed a great deal of value on their work, and Carlos and Steve gained a clear view into their impact. At the same time, they also earned a new standing inside of our organization, and senior executives recognized their leadership potential. Their self-confidence grew, and they began to receive more authority on other projects that followed.

LEARNING OPPORTUNITIES AND ASSIGNMENTS

Formal training can be useful in leadership development, when done right. Plenty of leadership programs provide experiential learning. Some require the sponsorship of your company.[72] You may consider sending employees to coaching training to sharpen their skills[73] or introducing them to Appreciative Inquiry[74] or positive psychology.[75]

72   SMU Cox School of Business, Cox Leadership Academy, https://www.smu.edu/cox/Executive-Education/Leadership-Academy.

73   International Coaching Federation, https://coachingfederation.org/about.

74   Center for Appreciative Inquiry, https://www.centerforappreciativeinquiry.net/certification/.

75   Positive Psychology Center University of Pennsylvania, https://ppc.sas.upenn.edu/.

At the same time, sending people to a few training courses may not be enough to help them achieve an understanding of what leadership is. They must also reflect on what they learn and also have the chance to apply their learning in real-life situations. Toward that end, you may consider giving them learning assignments.

Over the years, during regular meetings with senior managers, I would try different approaches. For example, I would decide not to discuss project-related activities, but to lead discussions on articles or books that I'd assigned the week before. One book I liked to assign was *The Second Mountain* by David Brooks.[76] The book focuses on living a life in service of others. The assignment I would attach to reading the book was for managers to write and share what resonated with them. Managers would share that reading the book made them reflect on their passions and examine where they found happiness or whether or not they were happy at all.

Whatever approach you decide to take, be sure to include time to discuss and reflect on various lessons in order to draw out what people learn. If people do not reflect, they may lose what they learn.

THE SPIRIT OF COMMUNITY

With the right mix of opportunities and mentoring, employees will find their way into leadership roles, thereby carrying your own legacy forward. But there is more to it than simply creating

---

76 David Brooks, *The Second Mountain: The Quest for a Moral Life* (New York: Random House Publishing Group, 2019).

an army of individual leaders marching to their own drums. If silos continue to exist, have you really left your mark?

A leader of significance must also find ways to create what I refer to as a social network, or a web, where leaders collaborate in order to benefit the organization and discuss how to enhance leadership skills.[77] You need to foster an environment where people move as a collective toward a shared vision. To build such an environment, you must continue to engage and find ways to build empathy and trust. This is the hallmark of creating a leadership of belonging.

Shared leadership builds the underpinnings and framework of a forward-thinking organization where many voices contribute to success. As you help individuals develop their skills, you must put in effort toward building a community of leaders. After all, you want leaders to grow together, learn from each other, and stay connected for years to come.

Even the most talented leader requires the input and leadership of others. Otherwise, you may run the risk of creating single-minded leaders who work in stand-alone ways. This may be good for them in the short term, but it does not benefit the organization or create a framework for long-lasting success. In fact, it lessens their own effectiveness, and it does nothing for your own legacy.

Forging enduring human connections results in leaders who not only have a sense of affiliation, but a greater sense of well-being. Building a community of leaders will also impact other

---

77 Catherine Robinson-Walker, "Succession Planning. Moving the Dial from Should to Must," *Nursing Administration Quarterly* 37, no. 1 (January 2013): 37–43, http://dx.doi.org/10.1097/NAQ.ob013e3182751622.

individuals in the future. These employees will begin to see that they are surrounded by peers who are dedicated to the success of the group. This builds social capital and a network of relationships that spurs cooperation, resource sharing, and new synergies. Once again, these outcomes cycle back into the organization, leading to more productivity and energy, and thus creating greater value.[78]

REFLECTIONS

Development is about enabling people to fulfill their potential, enhance and expand their talents, and go through life with meaning and satisfaction. As such, it embraces both training and education. It also involves coaching, listening, and internalizing what will help us and others expand our abilities to grow, mature, and perform.[79]

While I agree with Jim Collins that "Great vision without great people is irrelevant,"[80] developing other leaders can be tricky, complex, and uncomfortable at times. Still, the process is a rewarding one.[81] It is a journey of exploration, punctuated with moments of discovery. While on the journey, employees must maintain a growth mindset. While leading them forward, you

---

78 Isabelle Bouty, "Interpersonal and Interaction Influences on Informal Resource Exchanges between R&D Researchers across Organizational Boundaries," *Academy of Management Journal* 43, no. 1 (2000): 50–65, http://dx.doi.org/10.2307/1556385.

79 Joyce E. Bono et al., "A Survey of Executive Coaching Practices," *Personnel Psychology* 62, no. 2 (May 2009): 361–404, http://dx.doi.org/10.1111/j.1744-6570.2009.01142.x.

80 Collins, *Good to Great.*

81 Laura A. King and Joshua A. Hicks, "Whatever Happened to 'What Might Have Been'? Regrets, Happiness, and Maturity," *American Psychologist* 62, no. 7(2007): 625–636, https://psycnet.apa.org/doi/10.1037/0003-066X.62.7.625.

must continue to reinforce their belief in themselves and the importance of their effort.

In the end, you are the catalyst for other people's capacity and capabilities, and through them your legacy endures. You are not just supervising tasks, but you want the development of leadership capability of team members to be made of moments of significance.

As people develop their leadership capability, reflection becomes an essential element. It is how people discover and extend their insights and nurture connections. To get insights, people must believe that examination and reflection are worthy. Growth is the result of consistent investment of energy and time, and reflection. As an old Greek saying goes, "You suffer your way to wisdom."

As a leader, you have to walk others forward through a spirit of curiosity and help them discover insights that allow them to improve their leadership capabilities. You must also remind them to enjoy the journey of exploration. They have to believe that the journey is indeed an exploration. The theologian C. S Lewis talks about possessing an intuitive awareness when he writes of "the scent of a flower we have not found, the echo of a tune we have not heard, news from a country we have never yet visited."[82]

Indeed, growth involves stepping out of comfort zones.[83] This includes you as well. The path you take with others can help you

---

[82]   C. S. Lewis, *The Weight of Glory* (New York: Harper Collins, 2015).

[83]   Kaitlin Woolley and Ayelet Fishbach, "Motivating Personal Growth by Seeking Discomfort," *Psychological Science* 33, no. 4 (March 2022): 510–523, https://doi.org/10.1177/09567976211044685.

find your groove as a leader, reflect on your own strengths and challenges, and find new ways to articulate and communicate your ideas. Each development conversation is an opportunity for you to clarify the types of actions that will help followers move forward. You might even find yourself standing up to various shadow aspects of your personality. When you do, you will find many gifts waiting for you in moments of self-examination and exploration.

Developing others happens best within the context of psychological safety. When people feel appreciated and trusted, they will be more willing to take risks, knowing that if they fail, they will bounce back. When people understand that the resources and support they need to complete a task are nearby, they will persist in their efforts to achieve. It also fosters a feeling among employees of being part of a community. With this feeling, they will be more inclined to seek opportunities where they can assume leadership roles. This is yet another reason why it is important to create the context of psychological safety from which future leaders will emerge.

As employees develop their leadership capabilities, they gain recognition as leaders from senior leadership and stakeholders. What happens next is that senior leaders start seeking advice and suggestions from these new leaders. This results in new leaders taking on even more authority and responsibility as they develop.

Remember, leadership development is not an individual journey. Part of developing others involves finding ways to foster community and collaboration throughout the organization by promoting shared vision and common goals. You want to develop a community of leaders that grows and learns together. Doing so involves sharing power and information, which creates the feeling of "We are in this together," plus a better appreciation for the big picture and their roles in it.

Finally, it also requires that individuals are accountable for their own job. The process is not about creating a single figure, but a team of leaders.[84] You may indeed give some of your power away in the process of developing others, but do not worry about losing your thunder. What you are really doing is enabling a vision of shared leadership, thereby strengthening the future of the organization. When harnessed, these leadership qualities give the company a competitive advantage, improving organizational performance and cementing your legacy in the process.

LET US GET STARTED

Big dreams never materialize in a significant way through the actions of a single person working in a silo. Enabling others to develop their potential is at the heart of leadership.[85] You must take an active role in identifying and nurturing high-potential employees who are competent and motivated and possess the types of interpersonal skills that contribute to team building. These employees are committed to helping others grow and can emulate the leadership that you exemplify. As they win the hearts and minds of others, they create emotional connections and cement your legacy in the process. I would like to

---

84   Natalia M. Lorinkova and Kathryn M. Bartol, "Shared Leadership Development and Team Performance: A New Look at the Dynamics of Shared Leadership," *Personnel Psychology* 74, no. 1 (Spring 2021): 77–107, http://dx.doi.org/10.1111/peps.12409.

85   Shellye Archambeau, "Leaders Developing Leaders," *Leader to Leader* 2021, no. 99 (Winter 2021): 1–13, https://doi.org/10.1002/ltl.20553.

recommend the following actions to help you strengthen your competence in the practice of enabling others to lead:

1. **Be a coach and mentor.** Take advantage of any opportunity for coaching on a daily basis, helping employees discover new approaches to solving problems. Mentoring is a powerful way to develop other people. Assign new challenges that will take them outside their comfort zone, where they can participate in a profound way. Let them know how they can apply their talents in new ways. Identify and reward courageous behavior, and create an environment where high-potential employees can grow. To do so, you must stay engaged with them as they begin their own leadership journeys.

2. **Unleash leadership.** Model the way by leading the way you would like to be led. Share your leadership learnings. Become a champion of continuous learning in the organization. This helps build others up. Convey the expectations and responsibility for leadership across all levels, and be open about discussing how to take calculated risks. Direct them where they can get the necessary tools to further develop leadership skills. This may include books, articles, or formal training. Provide periodic reviews of their progress.

Chapter 11

UNLEASH ORGANIZATIONAL ENERGY

It takes a certain mindset to help mobilize the energy of employees and focus them on a particular strategic initiative, which is where I will focus Chapter 11's narrative. To do so, you must possess a deep sense of what you are attempting to accomplish and communicate the impact it will have.

Carlos Santana, the renowned guitarist, put it this way while speaking about a successful bandleader in an interview:

> You have to make a melody come alive, and be believable. At the same time, have enough confidence that you can lead like an alpha wolf. You need to lead the pack, which is the rest of the musicians, into a place that's not a desert, where you're not going to run out

of water. You're supposed to take the musicians in your band to a place where there's always milk and honey.[86]

In a similar way, employees will work independently to strengthen their own capabilities by tapping into their potential and enjoying the process. The psychologist Mihaly Csikszentmihalyi tells us that we get that feeling "when we are in a state of flow" that comes from a balance of competency and challenge.[87]

How does a leader create this type of situation? You begin to find your way when you shift the focus to your people and the organization as a whole. In this state, the work of leadership is no longer about you. It's about the collective moving as a single organism toward a shared goal and outcome. Channeling this type of organizational energy is what being a leader of significance is all about.

FINDING ALLIES AND ENERGY

Our company in North Carolina was not participating in a key market segment within the plastics and coatings space. Our formulations simply did not stick to plastics, and no one saw the need to pursue it. We were fine with steel, metal, and wood, so why push toward something new? Quietly, a number of us in leadership believed that we should be exploring a way into plastics. It was an adjacent market. By pivoting toward it, we would open many new possibilities. In addition, the plastics

---

86   Mike Greenhaus, "Interview: Carlos Santana Discusses His MasterClass on 'The Art and Soul of Guitar,'" *Relix*, March 6, 2019, https://relix.com/articles/detail/interview-carlos-santana-masterclass-the-art-and-soul-of-guitar/.

87   Mihaly Csikszentmihalyi, *Flow: The Psychology of Optimal Experience* (New York: Harper & Row, 1990).

segment was experiencing double-digit growth, yet we were on the outside looking in.

During a meeting one day, a team member named Mike Siegel mused, "What if we were able to get into that market?"

Oddly enough, Mike's seemingly rhetorical question was enough to get the wheels turning. "There are plenty of examples that suggest your idea has merit," I said. "It's not uncommon for a company to leverage their technologies and enter adjacent markets."

"Would we be able to do it here?" Mike asked. I encouraged him to continue to explore the idea.

The old adage "Where there's a will, there's a way" is a common one, but few people think of the inverse: "Where there is a way, there is a will." As I saw it, perhaps there was indeed a way. If we found it, would we be able to tap into our collective will? Or did it take more than sheer will? Our firm would need to engage our employees' enthusiasm and positive energy to achieve effort. How could I invoke their passion in a way that would encourage people to move in this direction?

Without question, moving toward plastics would be a challenge for our firm. Coating solutions for plastics required a primer, and most coatings in the market were solvent based, meaning they were not environmentally friendly. At that time, our firm's presence in automotive interior coatings was weak, and we possessed limited knowledge in that market. Plus, the demand was inelastic in this industry, and companies generally passed the costs of meeting regulatory demands to consumers.

It's not easy to get people to see, believe, and commit to an opportunity. One of the first things a leader must do is to find a way to turn an intangible concept into a tangible step or series of tangible steps. In essence, a vision must become concrete. Once it does, a leader's job is to champion the work of others in order to help them maintain their commitment and energy.

There was a big difference between conventional plastics coatings and the materials in which we focused, and figuring this out would be a major hurdle to overcome. In our R & D lab, Steve, an emulsions chemist, was already moving forward with a new processing technology that would allow us to skip the primer step and start with a top-coat application. This was an excellent and very tangible way to begin our work.

Two other team members, Dave and Kristen, joined him and focused on working with waterborne technologies in order to eliminate solvents. A strong sense of camaraderie began to form among them as they worked toward their shared goal. Each team member worked late and focused on investing as much energy as possible toward finding a solution.

At this same time, I sensed more organizational energies and excitement beginning to galvanize. Soon other enthusiastic team members jumped in, took active roles, and began to turn the effort into a mission. One colleague created and shared a document where he gathered thoughts and ideas about the market and gave people a chance to suggest ways that the group could test assumptions. This process was another step in addressing intangible uncertainties with tangible steps.

Eventually, we arrived at the moment when it was time to test the idea at a minimal cost. Kristen suggested that we find a company that was progressive enough to be interested in learning about the idea—perhaps they would work with us to refine it. We began assessing top-tier suppliers to better understand their market needs. It was around this time that one of our chemists attended a conference where a renowned scientist led a presentation on this very issue, including a discussion of market requirements. When the chemist returned and shared the news, we agreed that she should reach out to Dr. Rose Ryntz, the industry expert, and invite her to our labs. Our hope was that she would help us refine our process so we could make this critical business transition.

In the course of a few days, with Dr. Ryntz's help and guidance, we broadened our knowledge of the plastic markets and adjusted our formulations in order to meet the needs of the new application. This plastics coatings expert also proved to be an excellent networker and connected us with technicians at another firm. As more and more energy cycled into the process, it began to feel like a collection of protons and electrons gathering around a nucleus. Something much bigger was forming.

SCALING UP

Creating the solution in the lab was its own type of beginning. Once we had it in our sights, the question shifted to whether or not we could make it scale in a way that made business sense. We needed to conduct a pilot program to prove to leadership that our plan was technologically feasible.

Jan Ruhl, an engineer from our manufacturing division, volunteered to work with us. He scouted and rented the equipment we would need to install in our plants and put his expertise to the service of the project. This level of discretionary support went beyond his responsibilities, but he knew that the challenge could benefit the entire firm and was happy to lend energy to the effort.

Jan and his colleagues in manufacturing went about a series of tests over a few days. Toward the end of the week, my office phone rang. He was on the other end.

"I have great news," he said. "The tests were successful." I could not contain my enthusiasm at this news. This was exactly the type of data we needed to take to senior leadership in order to demonstrate the credibility of the concept. We presented the results to leaders of sales and marketing to see if they thought we had something they could sell. The VP of marketing pulled me aside after we had finished our demonstration.

"Mosongo," he said, "I believe we're on the right track. This has been a team effort, hasn't it?"

"Yes," I said. "In every way possible."

As sales and marketing went to work on messaging and value pricing, we hunkered down to bring the final product to bear. When all was said and done, not only did we successfully enter the market, but we did so with a product that proved superior to anything else that currently existed.

The product addressed a number of critical market needs for automotive interior applications. First, direct adhesion onto plastics without the use of a primer reduced the number of steps in the coating process. It was extremely eco-friendly, therefore addressing environmental regulations. What's more, the technology helped our company expand our manufacturing capabilities, which we leveraged in future production processes. Indeed, our firm would do much more than compete in a new market space—we would lead.

THE POWER OF ORGANIZATIONAL ENERGY

The success of this project came down to something that all companies strive for: a collective effort propelled by the energy of a motivated group of employees. We were no longer individuals, but a team that mobilized to create and achieve a common goal. The collective contributions that came from all departments exceeded the sum of individual contributions.[88]

At the same time, once our efforts were complete, the energy remained. A few months after the launch, an employee on the R & D side came to me and asked, "When is the next big project?"

"As soon as you wish to begin," I said. When I look back on this experience, I see that the organization was filled with unlimited potential, and this project was the key to unleashing it. And when I think back to my own involvement, what I remember most was watching their collective ingenuity and enthusiasm with amazement.

As a leader, you must capture and channel the energy and emotional excitement of your employees. One way to do so is to

---

88 Bernd Vogel and Heike Bruch, "Organizational Energy," in *The Oxford Handbook of Positive Organizational Scholarship*, ed. Gretchen M. Spreitzer and Kim S. Cameron (Oxford: Oxford University Press, 2012), 692–702, http://dx.doi.org/10.1093/oxfordhb/9780199734610.013.0052.

engage and focus their intellectual capacities toward achieving a collective goal. In the process, you must remember that individual energy is simply a precursor to the potential sum of organizational energy. This includes your own energy.

No one can truly measure the energy that exists in an organization. As the old saying goes, "you know it when you see it." Or, as I like to say, "you know it when you feel it."

I have seen and felt this energy in the presence of employees interacting, partnering, sharing, challenging, and pushing forward together. I have seen and felt it while watching people enthusiastically approach small tasks with a big picture in mind. Little by little, the energy becomes palpable. It shows up as joy on people's faces, satisfaction in their words, and even as intensity in their eyes when they arrive early and stay late, hungry to keep moving.

Being able to galvanize organizational energy doesn't happen by accident, and the type of energy that brings something new into the world must come from somewhere. Such an effort involves enabling people and teams to activate their dormant energetic resources. In the story I have shared above, the company saw the possibility but needed the will to move toward it. It is like a carrot hanging at the tip of your nose—within reach if you are willing to grab it.

People always get excited with new ideas. It's human nature. Looking back at this experience, our members of R & D wanted to answer big questions, while our marketing and sales teams were excited about creating new stories and opportunities to go to market. Something new is always a way to begin, especially when you are looking to build small wins or even just take small steps over time. However, newness only lasts so long.

Eventually, you must answer critical business questions and make the case that the work continues to matter, especially as months or even years go on. When the question shifts from "Why take this on?" to "Why are we still doing this?" a leader must be ready to maintain the momentum across the company.

Once you start going, maintaining a productive organization involves constantly monitoring the "battery level" of your people. How can you add more energy to a situation? When is it time to pivot toward the next step? Would now be a good time to cool things down over here and shift focus to there?

As you and your teams push forward with ideas, there will always be someone who is ready to step up, share the load, and even take the reins. Who are these people in your organization? If you are at the point where you are reflecting on your career, who have these people been? What roles did they play? How did they keep the ball moving forward? What work did they complete that helped turn an idea into something bigger?

To strengthen an organization's collective energy, you must develop a platform in which others feel safe and ready to lead. To do that, you must prepare them to lead. That way, they are ready when the time comes.

REFLECTIONS

Top athletes often speak of "being in the zone." For some, it is a tunnel vision phenomenon. For others, it is akin to entering an almost spiritual state of mind, from where they perform at their highest level. I used to wonder whether employees can experience the same feeling while working on projects. I have seen this happen many times before during my leadership journey. Still, how can a leader create an environment where groups of people at all levels begin to perform with an exceptionally high level of energy and productivity?

Reflecting on many success stories such as the one above, I believe that to galvanize and release this type of energy, the stakes must be high and the vision must involve something that the company has yet to achieve. People must believe that the work and effort will lead to an outcome that truly makes a difference. Otherwise, what is the point in the attempt? As a leader, you must promote the meaning behind the objective: how it will impact the company, customers, and even society as a whole.[89]

To start, I suggest selecting strategic goals that you and others in the organization see as opportunities to create an impact and deliver meaningful results. What you want to achieve must be clear, and the path forward must reinforce the notion that we are all in this together. Discuss how everyone's activities will help achieve something of greater worth and significance. Tell great stories that inspire and create a sense of meaning—something that can get adrenaline going and calls for participation. Be willing to go so far as to show them the future.

At the same time, there is a pragmatic side to this equation as well. Share the financials and provide the type of data that

89 Mihaly Csikszentmihalyi, *Good Business: Leadership, Flow, and the Making of Meaning* (London: Penguin, 2004).

people will rely on and trust more than anything. Then bring things together in a way that constructs the stories that exist behind and beyond the data. Above all, aim for actions that inspire and leave a lasting positive difference.

More than anything, you must empower people to be involved in setting the course. A great leader knows when to step aside. Be ready to allow your vision to evolve into a collective vision that changes with successes, failures, and new ideas. Let others take these ideas forward and openly participate in decision-making. When people decide for themselves, they are generally more committed to the results.

As an idea becomes a campaign, it will naturally transfer across other departments. In the process, you may find yourself offering guidance so members of other departments succeed as well. Support everyone on their journeys so they too rise higher up the ladder. Then, once the program is underway, continue to serve it and the people involved with your mind, heart, and fierce presence. Find creative ways to surprise and keep them motivated.

The collective social intelligence of a team is of the utmost importance. While energy can come from intrinsic motivation, it perpetuates, in part, from the day-to-day interactions between others. Maximizing collective intelligence depends on the emotional intelligence of team members. It is limited by the emotional intelligence of the least sensitive team member, while adding people with high social skills improves it.[90] You

---

90   Nicoleta Meslec, Ishani Aggarwa, and Petru L. Curseu, "The Insensitive Ruins It All: Compositional and Compilational Influences of Social Sensitivity on Collective Intelligence in Groups," *Frontiers in Psychology* 7, no. 7 (April 2016), http://dx.doi.org/10.3389/fpsyg.2016.00676.

may alternate individual and group work to maximize collective intelligence.

While individuals are more creative working alone, groups can combine ideas to improve further.[91] This means that in some cases, you may want to have the right mix of diverse backgrounds, experiences, and social skills, even if it means mixing and matching people as if you are conducting an orchestra, always ensuring that the dynamics of the group are positive and inclusive. This helps you recognize and get the most out of your energizers: those team members who motivate others and pull out greater performances.

When organizational energy is mobilized in this way, it enhances everyone's performance and becomes the hallmark of your legacy. Going forward, the company will never return to its prior dimensions. The energy reserve that you build is something the company can rely on for many years, whenever it needs to pivot, capitalize on an opportunity, or stave off a threat. Whatever comes, the organization and its people will know how to deploy the energy it needs to achieve the highest performance possible.

Here are some questions I'd like you to consider: Once you build something, can you continue to marshal organizational energy to support other strategic goals? Or will the energy burn out once a single project is finished? My own thoughts are that the energy will always be there. In fact, successfully applying the energy is self-reinforcing and expands the poten-

---

91   Douglas Guilbeault, Andrea Baronchelli, and Damon Centola, "Experimental Evidence for Scale Induced Category Convergence Across Population," *Nature Communications* 12 (2021), https://doi.org/10.1038/s41467-020-20037-y.

tial of the energy going forward. The cumulative effects of galvanizing moments become our lived experiences, even for an organization.

Still, much like an athlete or musician who enters "the zone," you and your teams will need intermittent recovery time if you want to sustain performance. Nothing in the universe expands continuously. There will always be moments of contraction and rest. Relish these moments, encourage your people to do the same—and then prepare for your next challenge.

LET US GET STARTED

The energy that exists in an organization has been accumulating since its earliest days. When people are energized by a new vision, stagnant energy begins to shift and percolate; new possibilities capture imaginations and emotions as employees engage with their true capacities and capabilities.[92] Suddenly, they begin taking actions that free them from stuck energy and harnessing the new energy as they march toward completing strategic goals.

This type of movement can unlock doors that lead to extremely productive and satisfying periods in the life of any organization. I would like to share one more group of actions to help you strengthen your competency in the practice of unleashing organizational energy:

1. **Build energy.** To unleash energy, you have to build it. This involves all of the previous practices I have shared, which

---

92 Rob Cross, Wayne Baker, and Andrew Parker, "What Creates Energy in Organizations?" *MIT Sloan Management Review* 44, no. 4 (Summer 2003): 51–56.

help promote the type of organizational energy that feeds people and breeds more energy in its wake. This comes down to encouraging employees to become the type of organizational citizens who collaborate, help others, and celebrate their accomplishments as a collective.

2. **Mobilize energy.** Decide what approach you will employ for unleashing and channeling the organizational energy. It could be a threat, such as bankruptcy, fierce competition, or disruptive technology. Negative energy such as fear or frustration can be channeled toward addressing such threats. It could be an exciting opportunity. Positive energy such as enthusiasm and excitement can be channeled to capitalize on this opportunity. In both cases, it requires a clear articulation of either the threat or the opportunity.

CONCLUSION

What people expect from organizations has not fundamentally changed, even as the modern business context has become more uncertain. One thing that remains unchanged is the human experience. We are social animals, complete with a range of emotions. We yearn for connections, seek belonging, and thrive when we engage with others. We desire personal growth and want to contribute to something larger than ourselves. Most of all, we want our lives to be an accumulation of exciting experiences and moments of significance.

As a leader, you must find a way to manage and tap into these life-giving human forces on your path toward changing things for the better. How? By capitalizing on the power of human connections, by helping others believe in their ability to overcome obstacles and achieve lofty goals, and by igniting the potential that exists in those who look to you for leadership so they perform beyond their own expectations.

I believe that a lack of engagement is one of the biggest, most daunting detriments that organizations face today. Without engagement, there is no motivation. Without motivation, there is no passion. Without passion, there is no desire, persistence, energy, or enthusiasm. What do we have if we do not have these? Very little indeed.

This book is not meant to be yet another weighty tome about management or leadership theory. Rather, my intent has been to advocate for a type of leadership that shows itself in daily moments and actions. In the process, my hope has been to encourage you to make the most of every leadership opportunity that comes your way and to create moments of significance that help others sustain their own personal and professional growth.

More than anything, I hope that this book has encouraged you to recognize the following: if you want to sustain something positive and lasting in an organization, start by looking inward, then focus outward on those around you.

With this book, I have shared a roadmap through stories I've drawn from my own leadership journey in various industries and across multiple continents. I have distilled lessons learned into useful, actionable practices, which will help enhance your leadership competencies. These exercises feed into and off of one another. My hope is that you see the synchronous associations that exist between them and achieve the crescendo that happens as you apply them again and again.

The actions you take in pursuing these practices could represent moments of significance for individuals, teams, and entire organizations. In the end, this is what matters. When woven together, the actions will help you build the intellectual capital of your organization and propel it forward. Such work and effort is not just feel-good stuff. Much of what I've shared throughout this book points to measurable, quantifiable outcomes.

When you engage, empower, and mobilize the collective energy of employees, new levels of performance follow. It is like turning on one light, then another, then another, until the entire room is lit. I have worked with a wide range of organizations in many countries. I have seen the impacts of these approaches—from leaders pivoting in their thinking, to employees growing more engaged, to productivity shooting through the roof.

When an organization is mobilized in new ways, it becomes a powerful engine that makes room for extraordinary things to happen. This, in turn, enhances the process of achieving collective goals and exceeding even the loftiest expectations. Most importantly, these changes point the way forward beyond the notion of "achieving better numbers" and into the terrain of sustained success.

I have no doubt that the dynamics between you and your employees and constituents are complex and unfold in a variety of ways. However, I am convinced that as you continue your leadership journey, you will continue to recognize the power of experimentation, pushing against norms and aiming toward something big.

This work takes a great deal of energy, but it is extremely rewarding. I hope that this book has introduced you to a range of new ideas from which you can draw. I am sure that some resonate more than others, which is fine. In the end, you have the tools and insight you need to know which ones align with the DNA of your organization, as well as those that will enhance the path you are on.

These days, when I run into former employees, they rarely mention the great products we created. Instead, they talk about the experiences we shared: what they felt at the time, where they were challenged, how they grew, and how those feelings of growth continue. My guess is that you are on your way in this direction as well. You have helped people see where they are and have shown them what the future state looks like. In doing so, you have also helped them connect with the things they value at work and in the world.

To be a leader of significance, you must impact people's hearts and minds. This is the key if you desire to leave something powerful in your wake—a tail that extends far into the future. In fact, your legacy includes the many trails you leave behind. It lives in the hearts of employees you have touched and also in the very soul of the organizations where you have worked. From these places, it perpetuates, informs the future endeavors your employees take on, and continues to have a multiplier effect and impact.

As I have dedicated much of this book to discussing other people, I would not be surprised if you have found yourself reflecting on people from across your career as well. Remember, the journey to becoming a leader of significance begins with you. Who are you? What are your core values? What is your purpose? What are you trying to achieve? When you align your actions from a clear purpose, the results are extraordinary. And when you affirm your values with those of the collective, you can build genuine relationships and truly move in harmony.

It takes courage to exercise this type of leadership, but doing so results in organizations where employees feel engaged, energized, and ready to move forward. If you have been fixated on numbers or projects or accomplishing tasks in a silo, now is the time to let that type of thinking go. That is one of the first steps toward becoming a leader of significance. As you shed the things that do not serve you, you prime yourself to elevate the human spirit and awaken the gifts in others that currently lie dormant. In the process, you will begin to pull people forward—not to "achieve better numbers," but to realize sustained success and lasting change.

I trust that you can do this. Take a small step today, then keep going. You are ready to adopt new thinking, transform your organization, make an impact on others, and create a legacy that matters.

Be a leader of significance!

ACKNOWLEDGMENTS

Leadership is a journey, and I want to express my deepest gratitude to all colleagues, associates, and friends who have joined me along the way. Your hard work, dedication, and willingness to grow and learn alongside me have provided constant inspiration.

Together we have built strong organizations and supported each other's development as leaders. In an earlier draft of this acknowledgment, I named many of you individually, and the list was long indeed. But I was concerned about inadvertently leaving out someone who has been valuable or kind to me. To all my friends from around the world, you know who you are. Our conversations and experiences are part of my journey and have influenced this book.

Many of you will recognize yourselves in the stories I have shared in this book. For that, I thank you. Leadership is not something that is bestowed upon us, but that which exists within each of us. It was an honor to serve you, and I hope this book will inspire others to unlock their own leadership potential.

I'd like to extend my deepest gratitude to the organizations that have provided me with the opportunity to learn, grow, and lead: Master Builders Technologies, SC Johnson, Reichhold, Asian Paints, PolyOne, and Phillips Carbon Black. These companies presented opportunities to test my skills and grow as a leader. I am particularly grateful for the tolerance and support I received, which allowed me to experiment and learn from my experiences. I am grateful for the experiences and insights I have gained while working with you.

I cannot help but remember the late Greg Bobrowski, who gave me my first opportunity to be a manager. I am grateful for the trial by fire, which represented my first leadership crucible. That is where I discovered that if you are not outside your comfort zone, you will not learn. I also discovered that leadership is in investing yourself in helping others, and this became my leadership raison d'être.

I am also grateful to the many individuals who lent their support during transitions from one organization to another and from one country to another when I first joined different organizations. Your support helped me experience positive energy, develop a new sense of purpose, and successfully navigate changes in the various settings.

I am fortunate to have had my journey intersect with two truly remarkable individuals, and I want to acknowledge them. The first is Akio Shoji-San: for his invaluable guidance and support in understanding the subtleties of Japanese business culture and for his long-standing friendship. Even across cultures, trusting relationships are a requirement for effective leadership. He extended his wisdom long after retirement. Thank you for your long friendship.

The second is Vivek Patwardhan: for his wisdom and guidance. As a guru and a counselor of values and experiential knowledge, he provided invaluable counsel during the development of the organization in India. No one person can possibly have all the answers or know how to ask the right questions.

In addition, I want to express my great appreciation for institutions that equipped me with the knowledge and resources to comprehend the complexities of individual and organizational behavior. In particular, the following three come to mind:

1. Case Western Reserve University and their organizational behavior program. Special thanks to Professor David Cooperrider for his lectures and workshops on Appreciative Inquiry, which heightened my emotional sensitivity for understanding organizations as living systems. Thanks to Professor Richard Boyatzis for his lectures on emotional intelligence, which helped to enhance my social and emotional competencies.
2. The International Coaching Federation, with their coaching trainings and seminars. I am grateful to Master Certified Coach Barbara Anderson, from whom I learned that art of coaching and how to enhance my presence to clients.
3. The University of Pennsylvania, with its positive psychology program: Professor Tal Ben-Shahar, with his lectures on positive psychology, helped me gain a better appreciation of the emotions, strengths, and virtues that promote success for individuals and communities.

I would like to extend my heartfelt thanks to the team at Scribe Media for their tireless efforts in bringing this book to fruition. I have been blessed to work with such a great group of professionals, who made the publication of this book possible. To Darnah Mercieca, who ensured the overall coordination and kept all the pieces working harmoniously. To Seth Libby, who helped give it shape from the very beginning. I am grateful for the able writing assistance from Dave Jarecki. Your thought-provoking questions helped me crystalize my thoughts. I am glad that we moved in the same rhythm. I also extend my thanks to Kelly Teemer, who orchestrated a world-class marketing campaign, ensuring that the book ends up in your hands. Finally, Susan Schultz, for her creative design of the book cover. I could not ask for better.

The journey could not have been possible without the love and support of my family. Working in different countries is challenging, and leading others takes energy and can be frustrating, so thank you to my wife for your love and sacrifice and to my adult children, Camille, Kambili, and Elali, for your love and the joy you bring to my life. I cannot possibly end this list of acknowledgments without thanking my parents for teaching me the sense of wonder and discovery, and giving me the ability to fly. I wish you were still here. Thank you.

And finally, to you. I hope this book serves to inspire you to embrace the leader within you and to strive toward your own personal and professional growth. Thank you for reading and sharing this book.

ABOUT THE AUTHOR

MOSONGO MOUKWA is a seasoned executive and consultant who has dedicated his career to helping companies thrive by commercializing new technologies, diversifying their product offerings, and entering new markets.

Across thirty-plus years in leadership, Mosongo has applied his unique talent for identifying leadership gaps and developing the talent and culture necessary for success. He helps solve important innovation challenges that hold organizations back by unleashing the collective creativity of their people. This results in increased profitability and growth expansion.

Mosongo has held leadership positions in R & D and operations at some of the world's most respected brands, including vice president, global technology at SC Johnson; vice president, global technology at Reichhold; vice president, technology at Asian Paints; director of technology at Avient (formerly Poly-One); and chief, global R & D at PCBL (formerly Phillips Carbon Black Ltd.).

In addition to his professional pursuits, Mosongo is a global citizen, having lived and worked in Belgium, Canada, the United States, and India. He is fluent in multiple languages and has led teams based in countries around the world. Mosongo is also an avid adventurer, having crossed the Arctic Circle as a member of the Polar Bear Chapter of the Order of Arctic Adventurers.

As a thought leader in leadership development and organizational change, Mosongo has shared his insights in interviews and articles for publications. They include interviews on leadership demystified with *Human Capital*, as well as a panel discussion on neuroscience, project management, and business moderated by Wanda Curlee of American Public University. His articles have appeared in *The Journal of Creative Behavior*, *Crain's Cleveland Business*, and *R&D Innovator*. Mosongo was featured in *Business Today* and is a regular contributor to *Business Standard*.

Mosongo holds a PhD from Université de Sherbrooke, Québec, Canada; a postdoctoral fellow at Northwestern University, Illinois; and an MBA from Case Western Reserve University, Ohio, US. He has been a keynote speaker at numerous international technical conferences and holds several patents. *Be a Leader of Significance* is his first book.